Better Homes and Gardens®

DECK & PATIO PROJECTS
YOU CAN BUILD

BETTER HOMES AND GARDENS® BOOKS

Editorial Director: Don Dooley
Executive Editor: Gerald M. Knox
Art Director: Ernest Shelton   Asst. Art Director: Randall Yontz
Production and Copy Editor: David Kirchner
Building and Remodeling Editor: Noel Seney
Building Books Editor: Larry Clayton
Contributing Architectural Editor: Stephen Mead
Remodeling and Home Maintenance Editor: David R. Haupert
Building Ideas Editor: Douglas M. Lidster
Remodeling Ideas Editor: Dan Kaercher
Kitchens, Appliances, Home Management Editor: Joan McCloskey
Associate Editors: Kristelle Petersen, Cheryl Scott
Graphic Designers: Harijs Priekulis, Faith Berven,
Sheryl Veenschoten, Rich Lewis

ACKNOWLEDGMENTS: Our sincere thanks go to the Western Wood
Products Association and to the California Redwood Association
for their help in the production of this book.

CONTENTS

ELEVATED DECK ALL-STARS

An off-the-ground deck can solve a multitude of problems—all the way from "leveling" a sloping yard to utilizing a hard-to-reach space. Selecting the right one for you may seem perplexing, but it needn't be. Not if you take some cues from the projects on the following 20 pages.

Each design deals successfully with a particular lot situation, and in doing so, adds a great deal to the beauty and usability of the house adjoining it.

You may find that one of the projects shown suits your needs exactly. More likely, though, you'll have to make some minor adaptations to make a design work for your arrangement.

Either way, you'll find the detailed sketch and directions (with frequent references to basic deck-building tips) accompanying each deck very helpful. They will guide you swiftly and surely to the successful completion of your project.

So, regardless of what your elevated deck needs are, you'll find help in this chapter. You know, there's really no reason to wait any longer for that deck you've always dreamed of having!

FUNCTIONAL: THE SHAPE MAKES IT HANDY

As an outdoor cooking center, this arrangement is a delight for both Mom and Dad. For her, it provides a sensible amount of room for preparing everyday meals on the counter next to the grill. And for him, it's perfect for those special occasions when he grills steaks or barbecues chicken. The location of the table makes this deck as cozy as an indoor kitchen and also convenient for serving meals.

Although an ideal site for intimate family times, this deck and patio combination can accommodate a big family reunion quite comfortably, too. There's always plenty of seating for family and guests.

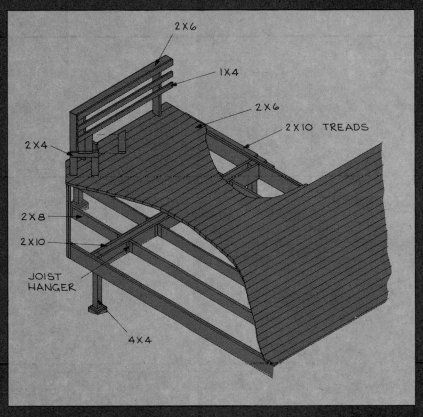

1 Study your site possibilities carefully and plan the deck to meet your particular needs (see pages 45-47 for ideas).

2 Stake out perimeter and prepare the site (see page 48).

3 Pour footings or set posts in concrete (see page 49 for details) and pour a concrete pad for foot of stairs.

4 Double-bolt 2x10s to posts as shown in the sketch.

5 Construct frame of joists and headers, connecting them to the beams with joist hangers (see page 49 for how-to).

6 Bolt railing uprights to the headers and outside joists (see page 57 for more information).

7 Construct the stairs shown in the upper part of the sketch. See details on pages 55-56.

8 Lay 2x6 deck boards (page 54). Cutting around the supports requires careful measurements.

9 Frame bench supports, attaching them to railing uprights and toenailing inner supports to the deck floor. Nail on seat boards.

10 Add the backrest boards and the cap for the railing.

11 Finish the deck, using a transparent preservative or an exterior-grade stain.

SUN CONTROL: THE ROOF SHADES HOUSE AND DECK

Here's a smart way to capitalize on a sunny, spectacular vista. The overhead cover gives plenty of shade while you're enjoying the deck at midday. And it keeps the sun's glare from intruding through those magnificent sliding glass doors as you look out. For further cooling effects, a planter hangs from the roof frame and a bank of evergreen shrubs skirts the base of the deck.

Without interfering with the line of sight, the low, open railing provides safety. And the stone edging adds the perfect finishing touch.

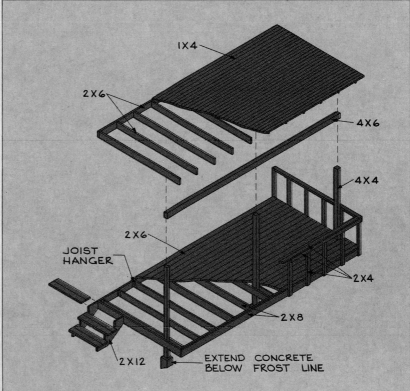

1 Get off to a good start by planning thoroughly (see pages 45-47).

2 Lay out the deck (see page 48). Then pour the post footings and the pad for the foot of the stairs (see page 49).

3 Anchor the 4x4 posts to the footings (see page 49).

4 Attach a pressure-treated 2x8 header to the house, using lag bolts into the house framing or expansion bolts in holes drilled in the masonry (see page 50). Complete framing by adding joists and outside double header as shown in the sketch.

5 Secure the 4x6 beam to the top of the posts using one of the methods shown on page 49, and build roof frame. Nail 1x4s ½ inch apart to the frame to finish roof.

6 Cut and install stair stringers (for details see pages 55-56).

7 Lay 2x6 decking boards and stair treads (see pages 54-56).

8 Construct 2x4 railing as illustrated in the sketch.

9 Finish with an exterior-grade stain or with preservative.

LOFTY: A COMMANDING VIEW WITH PRIVACY

This attractively imposing deck solves several problems at once: it adds lots of living space to a second story simply by serving as a giant balcony. And while it offers a splendid view of the swimming pool, the backyard, and scenery beyond, it also ensures a surprising amount of privacy because there are no stairs to permit traffic from below the deck.

As a bonus feature, this deck doubles as a sun roof for the area near the pool.

The use of massive posts and deep framing members overcomes the common pitfall of building high elevated decks with undersize lumber, which gives the finished product a tall, gangly look.

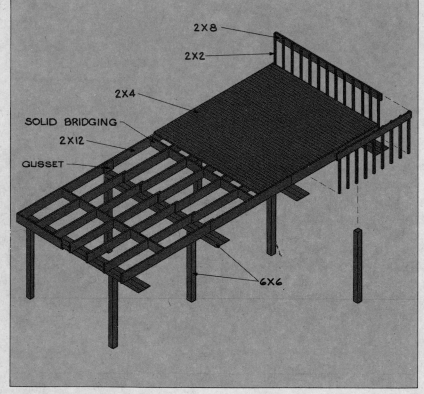

1 Make complete plans (see pages 45-47 for guidelines).
2 Pour footings, or set posts in concrete (see page 49).
3 Attach the beams to the posts (see page 49).
4 Set the 2x12 joists across the beams and anchor them by toe-nailing. Lag-bolt the first joist to the house (see page 50). Be sure to place any joints over a beam to achieve adequate support. Lap the joists where possible. Reinforce butt joints with gussets.
5 Nail headers to the ends of the joists.
6 Install solid bridging between joists to strengthen the framework (see sketch).
7 Lay 2x4 decking (see page 54).
8 Build railing of 2x2 uprights and 2x8s as shown in the sketch.
9 Finish with exterior-grade stain or with transparent preservative.

WRAPAROUND: IT GIVES A FEELING OF SECURITY

If your backyard has about as much privacy and atmosphere as an empty parking lot, transform it into a much more pleasant environment by building this stylish deck.

The redwood mini-deck offers a secluded, friendly spot for basking in the sun, reading, or just visiting. And the flowers and plants In the rock garden contribute to the relaxed atmosphere. Even the wooden "skylight" gives the area the feel of an outdoor room, adding to the sense of security.

But don't restrict this deck's use to only quiet times. Its large size makes it a natural for entertaining, too, and there's plenty of bench seating for everyone.

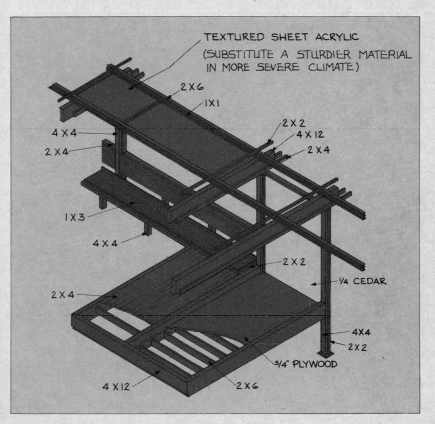

1 Start by working out a complete set of plans (see pages 45-47).
2 Pour concrete footings for the support posts, then attach posts to footings (see page 49).
3 Build the frames for the planter, mini-deck, and bench using the materials shown in the sketch.
4 Place the 4x12 beams on top of the posts, supporting opposite ends with posts or attaching them to the house (see page 49).

5 Complete the roof grid with 2x6 and 2x2 members (see sketch).
6 Nail lower 1x1s in place and install acrylic panels overhead. Secure with 1x1s nailed on top.
7 Install ¾-inch exterior plywood base in planter, and 2x4 redwood decking (see page 54).
8 Add bench surface and backrest, and install vertical divider of plywood siding.
9 Treat the deck with a transparent preservative, or use stain.

VIEW-FRAMING: A SMALL OVERHEAD DOES IT

One way to make a pleasant view even better is to frame it, as was done so beautifully here. The overhead beams and vertical columns define the perimeters, while the greenery complements the warm beauty of the redwood to bring the scene to life.

Although this Oriental-flavored setting is ideal for quiet relaxing, it's also large enough to accommodate groups for outdoor get-togethers or dining. The expansive wraparound bench provides plenty of seating, and the sliding door makes serving food easy.

Diagram labels: 2 X 12, 2 X 2, ½" SPACER, ⅜" THREADED BOLT, 2 X 6, 2 X 4, 2 X 10, 2 X 4, 4 X 4, 2 X 10, 2 X 12, 4 X 4, EXTEND CONCRETE BELOW FROST LINE

1 Double-check your plans by laying out your deck before starting actual construction (see pages 45-48).
2 Pour footings as described on pages 48-49.
3 Anchor posts to the footings (see page 49). Make sure posts that support overhead frame are long enough (see sketch).
4 Build frame as shown in the sketch, attaching one side to the house (see page 50).
5 Lay 2x6 decking boards (see page 54 for details).
6 Construct bench as illustrated.
7 Add overhead 2x12 and 2x10 beams, double-bolting them to the posts and attaching to the house with joist hangers. Fasten the 2x2 strips to the bottom of the 2x12s with long screws or ring shank nails to prevent them from falling (see sketch).
8 Apply a stain, or treat the deck with a transparent preservative.
9 Accent with your favorite plants and planters.

PRIVACY: TURN LIMITED SPACE INTO A HAVEN

Is your neighborhood one where homes seem only an arm's length apart, and where building a deck could put you on your neighbor's back doorstep? Don't despair! This freestanding deck idea makes excellent use of limited space and brings glamour to even the most uninspiring yard.

The deck floor serves as a natural extension of the adjacent room. And, stretching the area even more, the gently sloped stairs provide added room for planters or seating.

Build the screen and bench combination for those times when you prefer privacy, no matter how wonderful the neighbors are. It's attractive, airy, and with added lighting, it doubles as an outdoor den that's pleasant after dark, too.

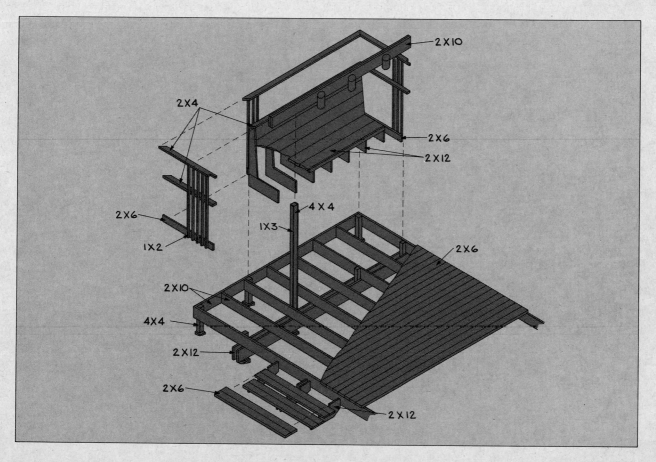

1 Draw up plans carefully, paying special attention to lot restrictions when building in close quarters (see pages 45-47).
2 Prepare the site (see page 48).
3 Excavate for the concrete pad at the foot of the stairs, and dig holes for the post footings.
4 Pour concrete for footings and stair pad (see pages 48-49).
5 Anchor posts to the footings and bolt beams to posts (see page 49 for the details).
6 Frame the deck as illustrated. For more on how to erect freestanding decks, see page 51.
7 Cut and install stringers for the stairs (see pages 55-56).
8 Lay decking boards and stair treads (see pages 54 and 56).
9 Fasten overhead beam to house with a double joist hanger and attach other end to post (see sketch and page 49).
10 Install light fixtures or hire a licensed electrician to do this job.
11 Assemble bench (see sketch).
12 Construct screen in sections, then attach to the bench, house, and support post.
13 Stain the deck, or apply a transparent preservative.
14 Lay plastic film or building felt in excavated areas, and spread pea gravel around the perimeter of the deck.

SPACE-EXPANDING: A NIFTY WAY TO HANDLE A SLOPE

Here, a stately old tree serves as the focal point for a charming deck that isn't connected to a house. You may have an equally appealing point of interest to build around, such as a boulder, a miniature fish pond, or a bed of shrubs.

Besides taking advantage of a site away from your house, isolating your deck makes it a fine place for kids to play.

This particular deck is an addition to an existing patio, generating more living space over a downslope. The low railing blends with the deck's contour without blocking the view.

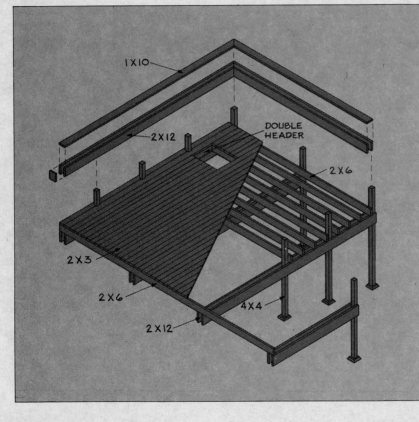

1 Choose a site carefully (see pages 45-47).

2 Dig holes for the footings. (In this illustration, one end of the deck rests on a patio surface.) Excavate and pour a concrete ledger along the entry side of the deck. Position the ledger so the 2x12 beams are flush with the patio surface. Or build it as a freestanding deck (see page 51).

3 Pour concrete for the footings, then erect posts (see page 49).

4 Bolt 2x12 beams to posts (see sketch).

5 Set joists across the beams and fasten them together with angle irons. If your deck surrounds a tree, frame a box opening around it. Do not attach any part of the deck to the tree.

6 Lay 2x3 decking boards (see page 54 for details).

7 Nail railing materials to the posts as shown.

8 Finish with stain or preservative.

BI-LEVEL: A PLEASANT TAMER OF TERRAIN

Making a sloped yard livable isn't as perplexing as it may seem. This deck features an upper level that runs flush with the main floor of the home. It's easily accessible and offers a full view of the yard. Up here, proximity to the house, with its wide eaves, gives shade and protection from the weather.

Take three steps down and you're on the lower deck for an interesting change in elevation. This section, which takes advantage of the slope of the ground, is a fine, level spot for lounging in the sun, and it's low enough to be safe without a railing. The 2x4 screen affords a measure of privacy, while stepping-stones form a unique path to the ground.

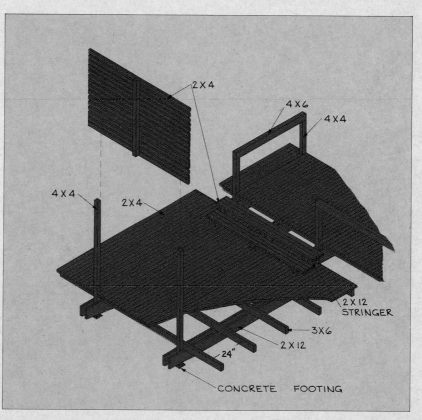

1 Plan both levels of this deck carefully, studying the change of elevation of your site (see pages 45-47). Examine the sketch on this page and the one on page 53 for a good understanding of bi-level deck construction.
2 Lay out the deck (see page 48).
3 Pour concrete footings, or set posts in concrete (see page 49).
4 Bolt 2x12 beams to posts (see sketch) and fasten ends of the beams for the upper level to a header lagged to the house (see page 50 for attachment details).
5 Toenail 3x6 joists to beams, or use angle irons.
6 Lay 2x4 decking, fitting it around the posts (see page 54).
7 Cut and install stair stringers and treads (see pages 55-56).
8 Add railing beams and the privacy screen (see sketch).
9 Apply stain or preservative.

EXPANDABLE: BUILD PART NOW — ADD MORE LATER

All too often, do-it-yourselfers run out of money or time (or both) when building the spectacular deck they want for dressing up their home.

A sensible approach to this problem is to construct a deck like this one: you can put up the main deck floor now, then add the end wall and overhead structure later as your budget and schedule permit.

Another expansion possibility is to build the deck as it appears here, adding extra sections or an adjoining patio later on.

The deck's low elevation makes it easy to modify with screens and other built-ins, too.

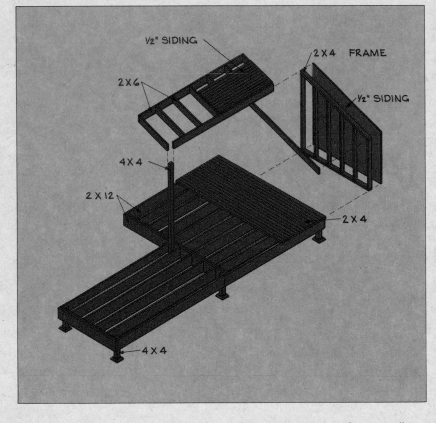

1 Plan the location of your deck (see pages 45-47) and lay it out (see page 48).

2 Dig holes and pour footings, or set posts in concrete (page 49).

3 Assemble 2x12 framing, starting with attachments to posts (see sketch). If desired, use joist hangers for added strength, as illustrated on page 52.

4 Lay 2x4 decking (see page 54).

5 Assemble framing for privacy wall on deck's surface, nail on siding, then erect wall, holding it plumb with bracing.

6 Build frame for roof (see sketch) and attach it to the house, the corner post, and privacy wall.

7 Nail lattice strips to frame as shown in sketch. If you live in an area of heavy rainfall, consider shingling the roof.

8 Finish the deck by applying stain or preservative.

SPACIOUS: IF YOU NEED PLENTY OF ROOM

For the clan with all kinds of activities going on, a large, rambling deck like this one can be a real lifesaver. There's plenty of room for playing games, eating, working on hobbies, and visiting—all at the same tlme.

This attached elevated deck will make a sizable expansion to the main level of your home. At this elevation, you're near enough to the ground to be comfortable, yet you can still get a feeling of closeness to the trees. And, from the deck or inside the home, it's easy to view the rest of the yard through the open-style railing that surrounds the entire deck.

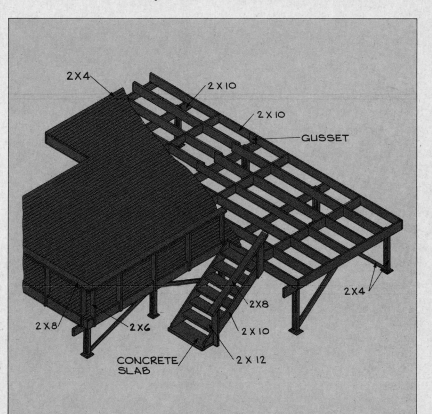

1 Plan carefully when working with an expanse like this. For guidelines, see pages 45-47.
2 Dig holes and set built-up posts of 2x4s into concrete, or pour footings and attach posts to footings (see page 49).
3 Double-bolt the beams to the posts (see sketch).
4 Assemble the frame of joists and headers as illustrated. Install solid bridging between joists as well as 2x4 bracing (see sketch).
5 Cut stair stringers and attach to deck frame as illustrated (see pages 55-56 for tips).
6 Lay 2x4 decking boards (see page 54 for more ideas).
7 Build railing for main deck and stairs (see pages 56-57).
8 Finish the deck with stain or a transparent preservative.

ON-GRADE DECK CLASSICS

Does your yard suffer from that wide-open-spaces look? Does it angle off at awkward junctures? Are there areas in it you haven't been able to put to good use?

If any of these problems sound familiar, then chances are, an on-grade deck will help you solve your landscaping problems and give you extra living space to boot.

Many of the designs on the next 18 pages are adaptable to any size or shape you decide on. And with some, you can make easy additions as your budget allows or as your needs change.

Not only are these decks good-looking, they're also easy to construct *and* to pay for. With some help from your friends, you should be able to raise any of them in a single weekend.

Detailed sketches and step-by-step instructions help make construction a breeze. Further pointers appear in the *All About Building Decks* section on pages 44-59.

SHAPABLE: TO FIT
AN IRREGULAR AREA

Deciding just what to do with an odd-shaped yard can be a real headache. In this instance, an unconventionally shaped deck turned a problem corner into a pleasant nook.

Rather than trying to force the usual patterns and lines into an unusual area, this design frames the deck with a combination of odd shapes, angles, and a curve.

The planter box and low railing add still another dimension and emphasize the irregularity of the deck's back edge. The result: a quaint, charming deck.

This one is a bit more intricate to build than many decks, but it's truly unique!

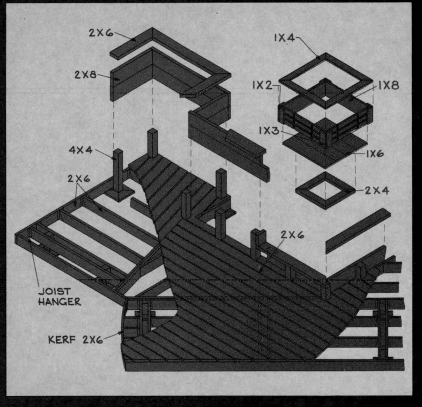

1 Planning and layout are crucial in building an odd-shaped deck. Study the planning points on pages 45-47 and lay out the deck beforehand to visualize the project (see page 48). NOTE: use redwood, cedar, or pressure-treated wood for members touching the ground.

2 Dig holes and pour footings, or set posts in concrete (page 49).

3 Construct 2x6 framing as shown in the sketch (see page 71 for details on kerfing).

4 Lay 2x6 decking (see page 54), fitting it carefully around the support posts.

5 Nail 2x8 backboards to posts as shown in the sketch, then add the 2x6 cap.

6 Build the planter as illustrated in the sketch.

7 Finish the deck with stain or transparent preservative.

ECONOMY: LOTS OF AREA FOR LITTLE MONEY

There's nothing very fancy about this streamlined deck, yet it adds a special appeal to an otherwise ho-hum backyard. But more than that, it's also one of the easiest and most economical decks you could hope for.

The low-slung on-grade profile makes this deck a comfortable transition between home and yard. And the chipped bark edging provides an interesting contrast—both in texture and color—with the house and plantings.

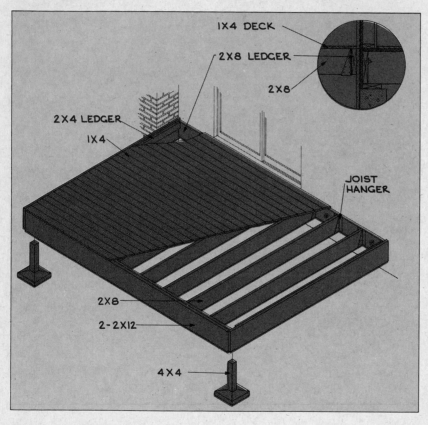

1 Select your site carefully and check your plans by laying out the deck first. See pages 45-48 for complete instructions.
2 Dig holes for pouring footings, or set posts in concrete (see page 49).
3 Bolt a 2x8 ledger to the house, then bolt the 2x12 outer frame joists and front header to the posts (see cutout in the sketch for details). NOTE: Use redwood, cedar, or pressure-treated wood for members touching the ground.
4 Install joist hangers 12 inches on center to receive the 2x8 joists (see sketch). Nail 2x4 ledgers in place on the outside joists, as illustrated in sketch above.
5 Install the 2x8 joists.
6 Lay 1x4 decking (see page 54).
7 Stain the unit, or apply a transparent preservative.
8 Add edging, potted plants, and other deck accessories as desired.

COVERED: ENJOYMENT COME RAIN, COME SHINE

With this deck, there's no need to grab everything and dash inside at the first sprinkle of rain ... or when the temperature rises ... or when the wind begins to blow. It's designed around the elements to provide you with long, uninterrupted hours of enjoyment.

In addition, the translucent acrylic side panels provide a measure of privacy while still allowing filtered light to reach plants and flowers.

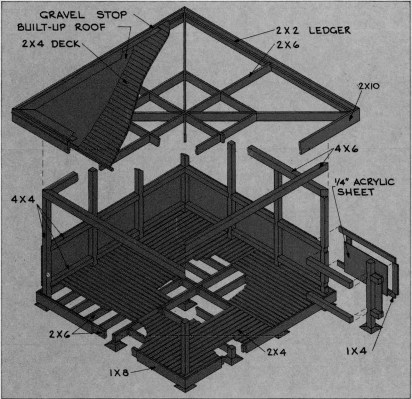

1 Give careful consideration to your site (see pages 45-47).
2 Dig holes for pouring footings, or set posts in concrete (see page 49).
3 Nail the double 2x6 beams to the posts as shown in sketch, then establish the perimeters of the deck by securing the outer 2x6s to the posts.
4 Use joist hangers to install the remaining floor joists.
5 Lay 2x4 decking boards (see page 54).
6 Nail 1x8 skirt to outer 2x6s.
7 Set 4x6 beams on tops of posts (see sketch; for attachment details, turn to page 49).
8 Assemble frame for the roof as shown in sketch.
9 Tightly lay together 2x4 decking for the roof and install the sheet metal gravel stop.
10 Have a commercial roofer lay the three-ply asphalt roof.
11 Nail 4x4 crossmembers between the posts. Use butt or dado joints.
12 Install the acrylic sheets, securing them with rabbeted 1x4s.
13 Finish deck with stain, or apply a transparent preservative.

MODULAR: SECTIONS GO WHERE NEEDED

This exciting deck is actually a grand conglomeration of identically sized mini-decks. Each of the modules measures 4x4 feet, and all are supported by a network of concrete piers sunk into the ground.

Because it's modular, this particular design adapts well to a variety of situations. And since each deck is easily removable, you can change the floor design at will, conceal hoses and garden equipment, or take it up to make way for a grouping of flowers.

In short, this design will do anything that you want it to—and at a price that's surprisingly affordable.

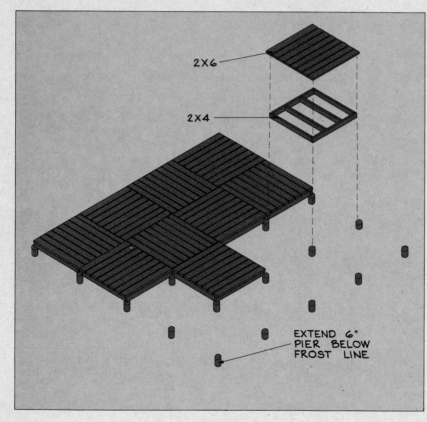

2X6

2X4

EXTEND 6" PIER BELOW FROST LINE

1 Examine your location carefully to determine exactly what area will be covered by the 4x4-foot modules. For planning pointers, see pages 45-47.

2 Placement of the 6-inch-diameter piers is critical. Lay out the area carefully (see page 48).

3 Dig holes for piers and place forms, using exact measurements. With a line level, check to make sure the tops of all forms are on the same level.

4 Pour the piers (see page 49).

5 Build as many modules as you need, following the sketch.

6 Position the modules on piers as illustrated.

7 Finish the unit by applying stain or a transparent breservative.

PETITE: TO UTILIZE A SMALL SPOT

If you develop them imaginatively, even those tiny "wasted" spaces in your yard can become islands of outdoor pleasure. A good example is this cleverly designed deck, which turns a steep bank into a handsome niche.

The structure is functional, too, providing an attractive passage from the paving-brick patio to the level below.

The inviting bench gives a furnished appearance, while the railing unifies the whole deck and incorporates an important safety feature. Judicious placement of the plants is the finishing touch.

1 Take a good look at your potential site, studying the change in levels to determine how the deck should be positioned. See pages 45-47 for tips on planning a deck project.

2 Lay out the deck to visualize the finished product (see page 48 for guidelines).

3 Prepare the site (see page 48 for step-by-step help).

4 Dig holes for the posts (see page 49 for more information).

5 Build the frame of 2x8s as shown in the sketch.

6 Cut and attach the stringers for the stairs (see pages 55-56).

7 Build bench as shown. For more ideas, see the *Project Dress-Ups* section beginning on page 76.

8 Lay 2x4 decking (page 54 tells how). Cap the decking board ends with a 2x2 strip (see sketch).

9 Install the stair treads.

10 Attach railing members as illustrated in the sketch (more information appears on page 57).

11 To finish the deck, use stain or a transparent preservative.

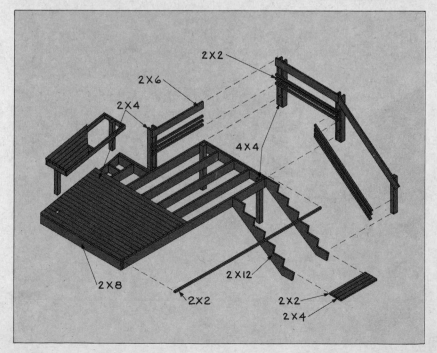

INTIMATE: FOR SOCIAL GATHERINGS

Conversation needn't be a lost art when your friends gather around this versatile deck. In fact, the face-to-face design and the centrally located fire-pit provide an ideal atmosphere for socializing around a flickering fire.

In the photo, this mini-deck is an offshoot of a slightly higher deck, but it can be equally impressive by itself. But for safety's sake, don't build it next to your house unless you omit the firepit.

The massive floor and benches are easily constructed of on-edge 2x4s with internal spacers.

1 Select your site (see pages 45-47 for details).

2 Lay out the deck to visualize the finished project (see page 48 for all the details).

3 Excavate the base area 4 to 6 inches deep and fill with a level bed of sand or pea gravel (see page 74 for help).

4 Assemble a decking base of 4x4s as shown in the sketch. Toenail the base pieces together. NOTE: use redwood, cedar, or pressure-treated wood for any members that will come in contact with the ground.

5 Lay 2x4 decking boards on edge, nailing together with ¼-inch spacers between. Also toenail to 4x4 base members.

6 Dig post holes and set posts for bench supports (see sketch). Bolt crosspieces to tops of posts and assemble seats (see page 57 for guidelines).

7 Stain the deck, or apply a transparent preservative.

8 Complete the project by lining the firepit with concrete block or native stones.

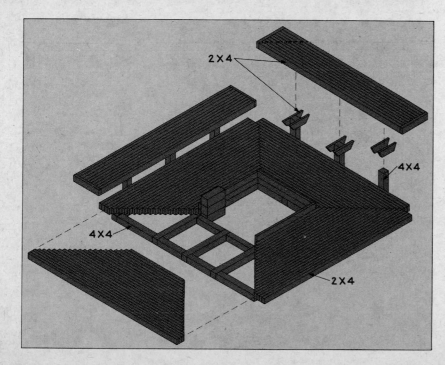

CONNECTABLE: THE RAMP OFFERS FLEXIBILITY

When you want to build a deck near the house but not adjacent to it (because of shrubs, trees, or other features you wish to preserve), separate the two and connect them with a ramp.

In this example, the deck is located under a tree, yet is close enough to be "connect-able" via the boardwalk. Even though this is an on-grade deck, it employs railings to define its boundaries and give it a sense of unity.

In addition to being decorative, the strategically placed shelves make an ideal serving center.

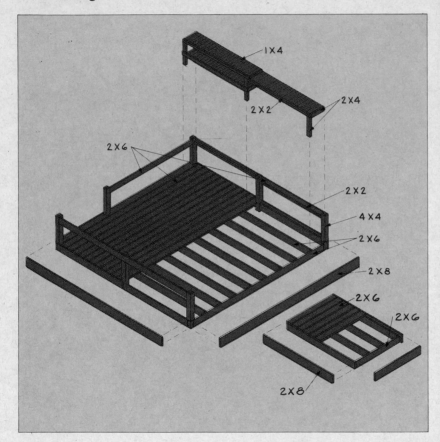

1 Carefully plan the location of this deck—its effectiveness depends on an appropriate site (see pages 45-47).
2 Excavate the base area 4 to 6 inches deep and fill with a level bed of gravel or crushed rock (see page 74).
3 Assemble 2x6 framework and posts (see sketch). NOTE: use redwood, cedar, or pressure-treated wood for members touching the ground.
4 Lay 2x6 decking (page 54).

5 Add 2x8 apron around perimeter of the deck (see sketch).
6 Install 2x6 railing sections.
7 Construct shelving units as shown. Add ledgers to railings, then secure shelves to the deck.
8 Build ramp to the correct length. Construction of the ramp is the same as for deck, using 2x6 framing and decking, skirted by 2x8s. Both deck and ramp sections float on a gravel bed.
9 To finish the deck, stain or apply a transparent preservative.

GRIDWORK: TAILOR IT TO FIT ANY SIZE

One problem for proud gardeners, when sharing their achievements with friends, is the awkwardness of having to stand up all the while. This mini-deck offers garden visitors a fine corner to ask about gardening secrets.

Moreover, the deck's handsome appearance complements its surroundings. And the color and texture of the wood, the pattern of the floor, and the elevated benches are all harmonious points of interest.

Here, the deck is a perfect square, but you can tailor the shape—and the size—to suit your own location.

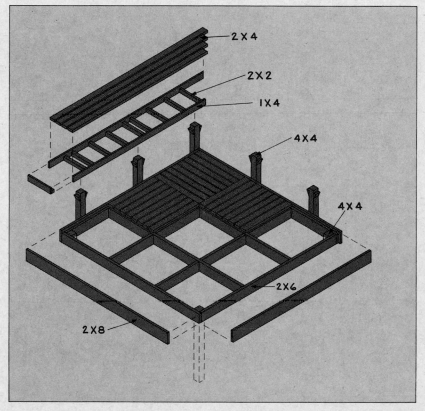

1 Choose your site to harmonize with your garden or other yard area (see pages 45-47 for planning ideas).

2 Dig holes for corner posts, making sure bottoms of posts extend below frost line. For a more permanent installation, consider setting the posts in concrete (see page 49 for details).

3 Construct the 2x6 framing as shown in the sketch.

4 Lay decking boards as illustrated (more deck-laying information appears on page 54).

5 Add 2x8 trim boards to deck's perimeter (see sketch).

6 Bolt bench support posts to two sides of deck frame (see sketch) and nail blocks to the upper parts of the posts.

7 Assemble frame and top of bench as illustrated. The finished seat should be 16 inches high.

8 As a finishing touch, stain deck or apply preservative.

SHADE-MAKING: TO HELP KEEP EVERYTHING COOL

If you're one who enjoys reliving the day's happenings with family or friends, you'll find this deck a great place to do just that. Although it is fashionably designed, the deck incorporates some of the enclosed porch design features that are reminiscent of days gone by...

The sloping overhead structure keeps things cool while it creates interesting lighting for the deck surface below. And the extra-wide 2x6 railing is a handy resting spot for food, beverages, or people.

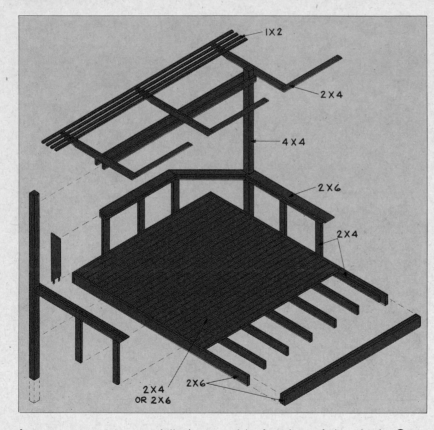

1 Choose your site carefully (see pages 45-47 for planning tips).
2 Lay out the deck and prepare the site (see page 48).
3 Dig post holes and set the posts in concrete (see page 49).
4 Assemble 2x6 frame as shown in sketch, and bolt it to posts and to framing of house (see attachment details on pages 49-50).
5 Lay 2x4 or 2x6 decking (see page 54).
6 Bolt railing uprights to the outside framing of the deck. Complete railing by bolting 2x4s to the uprights and nailing on a 2x6 cap.
7 Bolt 2x4 crosspieces to the posts that support the 1x2s. Drill and bolt together remainder of frame as illustrated. Fasten the upper end of the overhead to the house with framing anchors.
8 Nail the 1x2s to the frame as shown in the sketch.
9 Finish the deck with stain or a transparent preservative.

REMOTE: A REFUGE
FOR QUIET TIMES

Have an especially eye-appealing spot in your yard that you'd like to make super-special? Consider this easy-build deck.

Adding a simple platform like this banishes such annoyances as getting grass stains on clothes or sitting on damp soil beneath trees. Instead, the entire scene becomes a delightful place to read, daydream, or enjoy a few solitary moments.

The deck itself rides on beams that rest the ground. Its surface opens around the trees so that with potted plants added, the project resembles a giant-sized planter—but with plenty of space for plant-loving visitors.

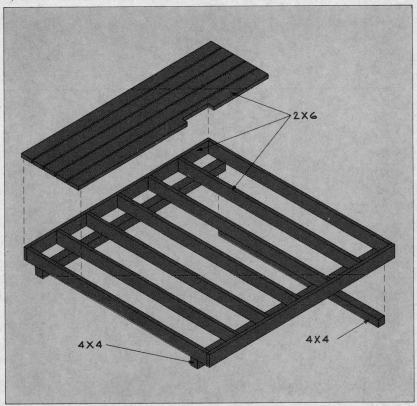

1 Put plenty of thought into developing your plans and selecting the site. A single tree, a shrub, a large rock, or some other interesting object can serve as a point of interest for your deck (see pages 45-47 for planning guidelines).
2 Lay out the deck to visualize the finished product (see page 48 for instructions).
3 Position the 4x4 base beams (see sketch). If you're building on level ground, only two beams are needed. NOTE: Use cedar or pressure-treated wood for members touching the ground.
4 Construct the frame of 2x6s as illustrated in the sketch.
5 Lay decking boards (see page 54). Fit them closely to tree trunks, but do not attach them to trees.
6 Stain or apply preservative.

TERRACED: TO FOLLOW A GENTLE SLOPE

Coming up with the right deck for a gentle incline can be a real skull-splitter. The solution may well be a simple terraced on-grade deck like this one.

Though it's a mere 9½ inches off the ground, it provides a nice, smooth floor with a striking appearance. And the bench in the rear serves as a highly functional third tier.

The floor packs some utilitarian surprises of its own—there's well-ventilated horizontal storage hidden under each section for tucking away garden and yard tools, hoses, and other paraphernalia.

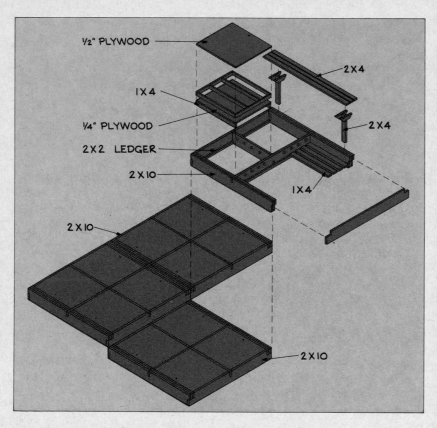

½" PLYWOOD

2X4

1X4

¼" PLYWOOD

2X4

2X2 LEDGER

2X10

1X4

2X10

2X10

1 Select your site carefully (see pages 45-47 for guidelines).
2 Lay out the deck to visualize the finished project (see page 48 for details).
3 Prepare the site (see page 48 for details). Some excavating and leveling of fill dirt may be necessary as you proceed.
4 Liberally treat all lumber and plywood with a wood preservative such as penta. Since the structure rests directly on the ground, this step is crucial.
5 Assemble 2x10 frame sections, drilling holes to permit cross ventilation (see sketch).
6 Install ledgers and 1x4 slats in storage areas. Leave ¼- to ½-inch spaces between slats.
7 Build floor frame for each section, then sandwich the frames with plywood and 1x4 stops (see sketch).
8 Build the bench (see sketch).
9 Finish deck as desired.

ALL ABOUT BUILDING DECKS

You want a deck, but building one scares you, right? Well, don't let it! You can do the job yourself without calling in a building contractor, without spending a fortune (in money or your spare time), and without all kinds of expensive tools. Just read the next 16 pages for all the basic know-how you'll need to begin building your dream deck with confidence.

Sound easy? It really is! Most decks, even the elaborate-looking ones, are well within the skill level of the average do-it-yourselfer. In fact, if you can handle a saw, a hammer, and a few other basic carpentry tools, there are very few you can't build. Just choose the plan that fits your home, your family, and your pocketbook, and you're all ready to begin!

STARTING OUT RIGHT

Certainly, the construction stage of your deck-building project is important. But it's the care and attention you give to planning the job that makes the difference between a successful deck-raising and one plagued with headaches. To keep everything on the right track, consider these first steps.

Check Lot Restrictions

Adding a deck to your home is like driving a car—there are certain rules you must follow. Failing to comply could result in your having to remove what you've worked hard to build.

Zoning regulations normally require homes, outbuildings such as garages and sheds, and other lot structures to be a specified distance from the property line. This distance is called the "setback" requirement. The sketch below shows typical setbacks.

First, verify the location of your property lines. You can do this by locating the corner markers. Don't guess! If necessary, hire a surveyor.

Next, contact your tax assessor, town clerk, or building office for information about local zoning regulations. If possible, get a copy to keep for reference.

Check your property deed, too. It may include an easement that gives others permission to use part of your property for a specified purpose. For example, a previous owner may have granted an easement to bury a water line under your property. This would also permit access for possible servicing. If so, you wouldn't want to build in the area specified.

Also check locations of underground utilities. If you have a septic system, make sure you know where it is. Locate water lines, sewers, and buried gas, electric, or telephone lines, too. Call your utilities for these locations and ask how deep the various lines are buried. It's wise to avoid building over them.

Building codes also can affect your plans. Often, these specify minimum requirements for materials such as posts, beams, decking, and railing structures. These regulations may very well do your "engineering" for you.

If you're in doubt about any of these restrictions, ask questions until you have answers. Be ready to show building officials your plans to confirm that your proposal is acceptable.

Plan for Privacy

Many otherwise serviceable decks fall into disuse because of a crucial oversight—lack of privacy. No one is comfortable when on display, so be sure to consider the following angles.

First, you'll want to avoid such annoyances as street noise, the roar of air conditioners, and unwelcome pets. The sketch at right shows how to use trees, a hedge, and a privacy fence to muffle traffic sounds on a corner lot.

To make your deck visually private, locate it on the back or the least exposed side of your home. Both sketches at right show how you can place shrubs and fences to ensure privacy.

If you have children, they're sure to see your deck as an inviting play area to jump, thump, and bump around on. Fine for them, but such percussive antics may shatter everyone else's nerves. So, you may want to locate your deck away from the house.

Consider the Climate

The north and east sides of a home are generally "cool" because they benefit from shade in the afternoon and evening. If you live in a mild climate, you'll probably want to take advantage of this shade.

The south and west sides of the house may be too hot for comfort unless you provide some protection from the sun. On the other hand, their cheery warmth may give your deck more days of use in the spring and fall, especially in the North.

Other factors you'll want to take into account are wind, rain, and snow. A gentle breeze can be refreshing on a summer evening. But brisk winds blowing in off the ocean or a large lake will bring an unwelcome chill.

And if you live in a region where strong winds occur, anchor the deck securely to keep it from floating off its footings.

Observe the usual direction of rainfall, too. If you live in a wet climate, you'll want a roof to shed water, and perhaps some protection to keep rain from blowing in from the sides.

Also, the weight of several inches of snow can crush even well-designed decks. So, if you live where heavy snowfall is common, consult building officials, materials dealers, or an engineer to make sure your proposed deck will be strong enough.

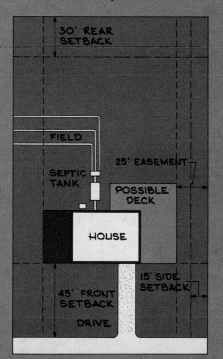

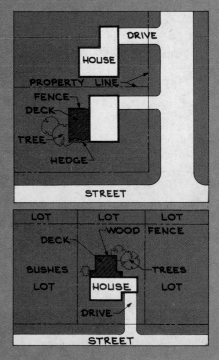

Plan for Function

How will you use your deck? As a spot to relax and cool your heels? To grill steaks? To sunbathe? To throw a party? More than likely, you'll use it for several of these activities. So, for a deck that's custom-tailored to your life-style, keep these points in mind:

Size. For a minimum of elbow room, allow approximately 20 square feet of floor area per person. Multiply this by the largest number of people likely to occupy your deck, and you have a good size guideline. You may need to adjust that figure to stay in line with the space that you have available and to keep the deck in scale with the rest of your home.

Furnishings and accessories. As a living area, your deck should be appropriately furnished with benches, tables, and other outdoor furniture accessories. For example, if you enjoy outdoor cooking, you may wish to build in supports for a grill. Or, if you expect to entertain large groups, you'll want to consider built-in seating.

Safety. An unexpected tumble, even from a height of a foot or two, can be serious. That's why building codes often specify deck and stair railings to be at least three or four feet high. As you work out your plans, make sure all protective structures are sturdy, and childproof them for toddlers if necessary.

Access. The easier you can move from the kitchen, dining room, or family room to your deck, the more you'll enjoy it. The sketches on this page offer ideas for dealing with different situations.

. In the top sketch, an existing side entry provides access to a deck attached to the rear of the home, as does a patio door in the living room wall. This arrangement makes meal serving fairly easy. But you could improve on it by adding a pass-through to the kitchen window.

The middle sketch shows a popular arrangement in which a sliding glass door divides dining room and deck. Stairs descend from the deck to the yard.

How about a freestanding deck? The one in the bottom sketch is neatly bridged to an existing kitchen entrance.

Tailor the Deck To Your Situation

Some deck designs fit certain homes better than others. The sketch at right shows the more common alternatives. Notice that the surface of the deck is usually at about the same level as the floor of the adjoining room. This makes it easy to move from one to the other, and also lets the deck appear to be an extension of the adjacent room.

So, if you have a two-story home and want your deck to adjoin an upstairs room, simply build it up on tall posts, as shown in the upper left drawing. An identical arrangement works for the split-level home, where the deck isn't as far above the ground.

Want to add a deck to a ranch-style home? Easy! An on-grade deck lifts you up off the ground, but, as the sketch shows, not so high that you need to build a railing for the deck.

For sloping yards, fit your deck to the terrain as illustrated. On an up-grade, consider a free-standing deck, attached with stairs and a landing. Or, reach out over a downslope with an elevated deck.

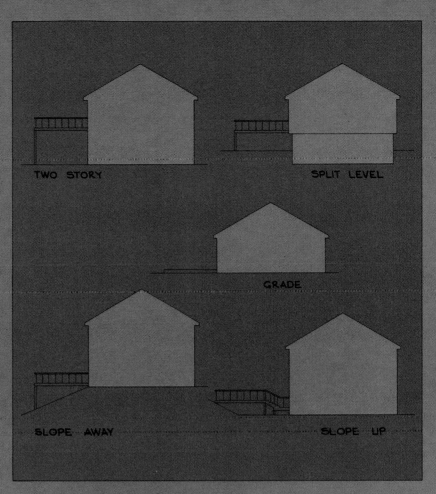

TWO STORY SPLIT LEVEL GRADE SLOPE AWAY SLOPE UP

Estimate Material Needs

Once you've decided on the type of deck to build, its dimensions, and shape, you're ready to estimate the materials you'll need.

One good approach is to draw a simple sketch of the parts of the deck—the footings, the posts and beams that will support it, the framework and joists, deck boards, rails, and the various stair components.

Drawing to scale will help you visualize the proportions of the deck. Use graph paper with ¼-inch divisions for a scale of ¼ inch per foot.

First, plan the placement of the footings. The distance between footings will depend on the size of the beams spanning them. Use the beam span table at right for guidelines.

Estimate your concrete needs from the number of footings to be poured and their dimensions, including depth. For more information on working with concrete, see page 87.

Posts are normally 4x4 or 6x6, the latter for heights exceeding 8 feet. You may wish to use larger size posts and beams for a more pleasing visual effect, but it's critically important that you keep them in scale with other elements of the deck.

Select the size for joists and headers (the boards extending across the ends of the joists) on the basis of suitable spanning strength. Consult the joist span table for help in determining your needs.

Decking boards usually are 2-inch-thick lumber, purchased in standard 2-, 4-, or 6-inch widths. Deck boards wider than 6 inches tend to warp, making them unsuitable for outdoor use.

In estimating decking board requirements, remember that 2x4s are 3½ inches wide, and 2x6s are 5½ inches wide. And allow ⅛ to ¼ inch spacing between boards (this prevents moisture buildup and subsequent rotting).

See pages 55 through 57 for details on building railings and stairs. When you've determined which style you want to build, you can estimate the materials you'll need.

Organize your list by dimension and length. List posts first. Follow with beams, joists, decking boards, and materials for stairs and railings.

Also jot down the hardware you'll need—joist hangers, nails, bolts, and other fasteners. And include your cement needs, too.

BEAM SPAN TABLE

Beam Size	Maximum Span
4x4	4 ft.
4x6	6 ft.
4x8	8 ft.
3x10	9 ft.
4x10	10 ft.
4x12	12 ft.

Place beams on edge for use

JOIST SPAN TABLE

Joist Size	Distance between joists		
	16 in.	24 in.	32 in.
2x6	8 ft.	6 ft.	5 ft.
2x8	10 ft.	8 ft.	7 ft.
2x10	13 ft.	10 ft.	8 ft.

LAYING OUT YOUR DECK

Sketching a plan for your deck permits you to visualize it and to estimate the materials you'll need. But the acid test comes when you transfer the planned dimensions to your intended site. If your plan isn't right, you'll find out about it now, before you've ordered your materials.

Stake the Perimeter and the Footings

Start by locating one corner adjacent to the house. Drive your first stake at that point. Measure the length of the deck and drive a second stake, also adjacent to the house. From either of these stakes, measure off the width of the deck, following a line perpendicular to the wall of your home (see sketch below).

Drive the first outside corner stake just deep enough to anchor it; you may have to reposition it later. Locate the fourth corner by measuring the length and width from the appropriate stakes. Then stretch a chalk line or string around these stakes for a visualization of the finished size and to serve as an excavation guide.

Measure and mark the location of each post, and drive a stake to mark the center of each one.

Square Up the Corners

For best appearance and maximum strength, rectangular decks must have corners that form perfect right angles. To ensure that your layout is square, use the 3-4-5 system, illustrated at right. Any multiple of these dimensions such as 6-8-10 or 9-12-15 will also work. Here's how to use it: from a corner, measure 3 feet along the back and 4 feet along one end. If the layout is square, the diagonal or hypoteneuse will be 5 feet. If it isn't, adjust the stakes until the diagonal measures 5 feet.

A quick way to double-check the squareness of your layout is to measure the distance between opposite corners. If they are equal, the layout is square.

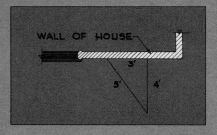

Prepare the Site

Unless your deck will be a full story tall, the area underneath it will be shaded and therefore unsuitable for grass and most ground covers. So, you may as well salvage the sod by taking it up with a spade or sod cutter, as shown in the sketch above. You can then use it to repair bare spots elsewhere in your lawn.

Next, dig holes for footings or posts. These should reach below the frost line to prevent movement from freezing and thawing of the soil. This depth varies all over the country, so ask a builder or concrete supplier for help.

To prevent weeds from growing under your deck after it's finished, cover the bare dirt with heavy black plastic (polyethylene film), and top with crushed stone, pebbles, or bark for best appearance.

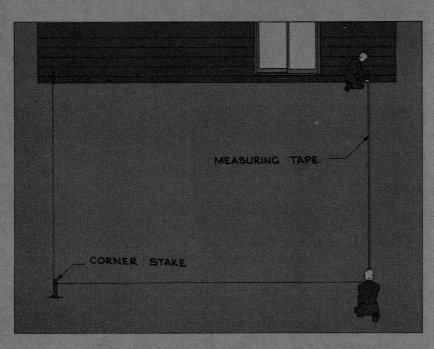

MEASURING TAPE

CORNER STAKE

SETTING THE POSTS

Because they are the cornerstones of your deck, the posts deserve extra attention. More than a few decks have suffered an early demise because of posts that rotted away. This needn't happen!

There are two acceptable ways to set deck posts. The first involves setting the posts directly into concrete as the sketch below shows. This is a typical installation using a cylindrical waxed fiber form. You can buy these forms in several diameters and cut them with a handsaw to whatever length you need. Make sure the bottom of the post rests on top of 5 or 6 inches of concrete and that the concrete collar extends at the very least 2 inches above ground level.

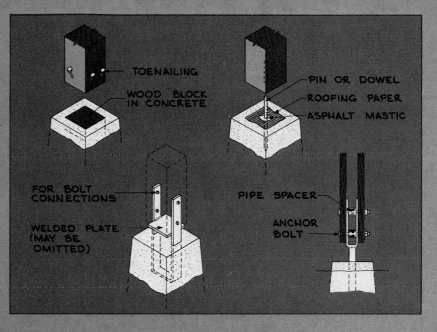

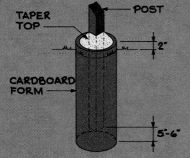

The other—and preferred—method is to use concrete footings. In firm soil, you can dig holes that can double as forms

below the soil's surface. Above ground, you'll need to put up forms for pouring concrete pedestals, which protect posts from moisture, rot, and insects.

The sketch above shows several ways to anchor posts.

When setting the posts—either in concrete or on top of footings—make sure they are plumb and aligned with each other. Use a carpenter's level to check for perpendicularity. Check each post twice, making readings on sides at right angles to each other.

Drive sturdy stakes, and nail outrigger braces in place to keep posts plumb until the concrete hardens (see sketch at right).

Where posts rest on footings, bracing will hold them plumb during construction.

ATTACHING THE BEAMS

At the house wall, tack one end of a leveling line where the surface of the deck will be. With line level taut, locate the same height on one of the posts. Subtract the combined thicknesses of a deck board, joist, and beam to establish the correct level of the post tops. Mark this level on all of the posts and saw each of them off evenly.

After resting the beam on top of the posts, use one of the methods shown in the sketch at right to fasten them together. Bolted joints make the strongest possible connection.

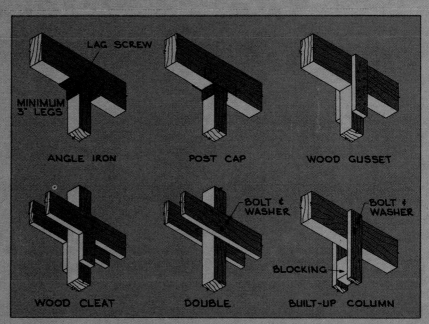

BASIC DECK CONSTRUCTION DETAILS

Seeing exactly how all the parts fit together takes the mystery—and the fear—out of building your own deck. Actually, deck construction is quite easy, as you'll see after studying the next four pages.

You'll also notice that the major types of decks have a great deal in common. For example, erecting the posts and beams usually is pretty much the same. So is assembling the framework of joists and headers, which go together much like the structure that supports the floors in your home.

Where differences between decks do exist—such as the various ways of attaching a deck to your house—the detailed drawings presented on these pages make them easy to understand and deal with.

Attached Elevated Deck

In this example, the house supports one side of the deck and posts hold up the other. For a long joist span, add an intermediate post-and-beam assembly to support the middle (see the joist span chart on page 47 for help in determining your needs).

You can use either of the two methods shown to fasten the deck to the house. With the top method, you extend bolts through the header on the deck, and the siding, sheathing, and header on the house.

Your other choice is to bore holes in the concrete foundation, insert lead or plastic expansion plugs, and attach a ledger with lag bolts. Then nail ledger, blocking, and deck header together.

Notice, too, how the ledgers and inside joists support decking boards so that the completed surface is flush with the upper edges of the end joists and header. This contributes to a clean, finished appearance. Solid bridging adds strength to the frame.

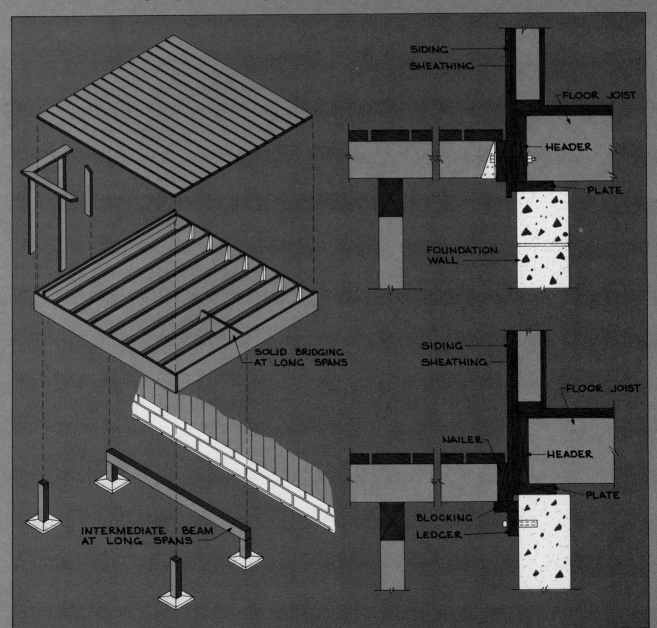

Freestanding Elevated Deck

Here's a deck that literally stands on its own feet. You can build it anywhere—adjacent to your home or if you'd rather, in a nice, shady corner in the backyard.

But that's not all this type of deck has going for it. It's easy to construct because you don't have to hitch it to your home. And because the deck isn't physically touching the existing structure, moisture buildup isn't a big worry, either.

To build this one, set posts in concrete and build up beams by bolting heavy boards to opposite sides of the posts. The cutout at right shows you how.

Nail solid bridging between the joists. This prevents the joists from twisting and distributes the load over the whole deck.

The joists reach beyond the beams and hide the posts underneath. Lay decking boards on top of all joists and evenly cut off the ends. Then attach rail balusters to the header and the end joists, add rails, and you're through with your project!

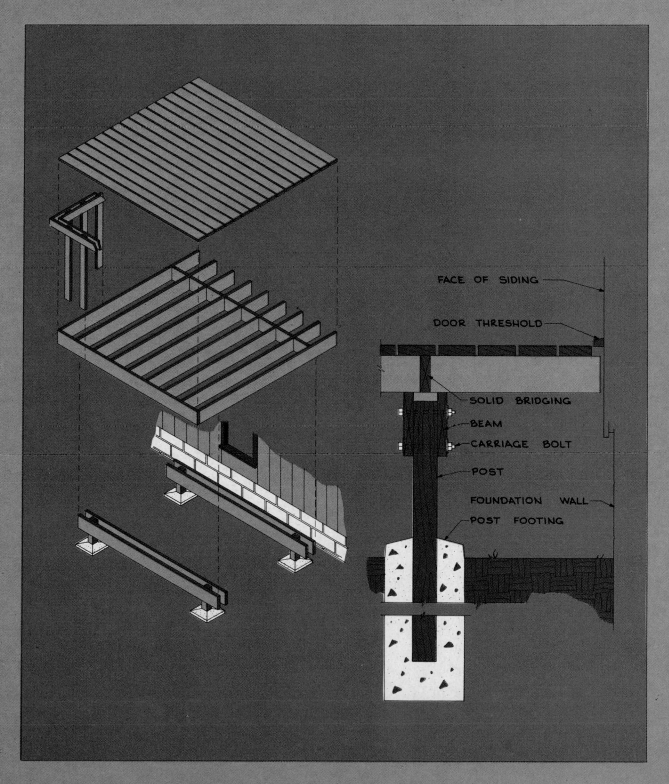

FACE OF SIDING

DOOR THRESHOLD

SOLID BRIDGING

BEAM

CARRIAGE BOLT

POST

FOUNDATION WALL

POST FOOTING

On-Grade Deck

Like sheer simplicity? Then take a look at this beauty. It's nestled close to the ground, resting on four corner posts. Or, if you like, you can easily anchor this deck to your house and erect posts only at the outside corners. The size is up to you—all the way up to a whopping 20 x 20 feet.

Install joist hangers to strengthen the joints between the headers and joists. Then fit decking boards inside the framework so that their ends won't show. Since this deck is on-grade, there's no need to equip it with railings.

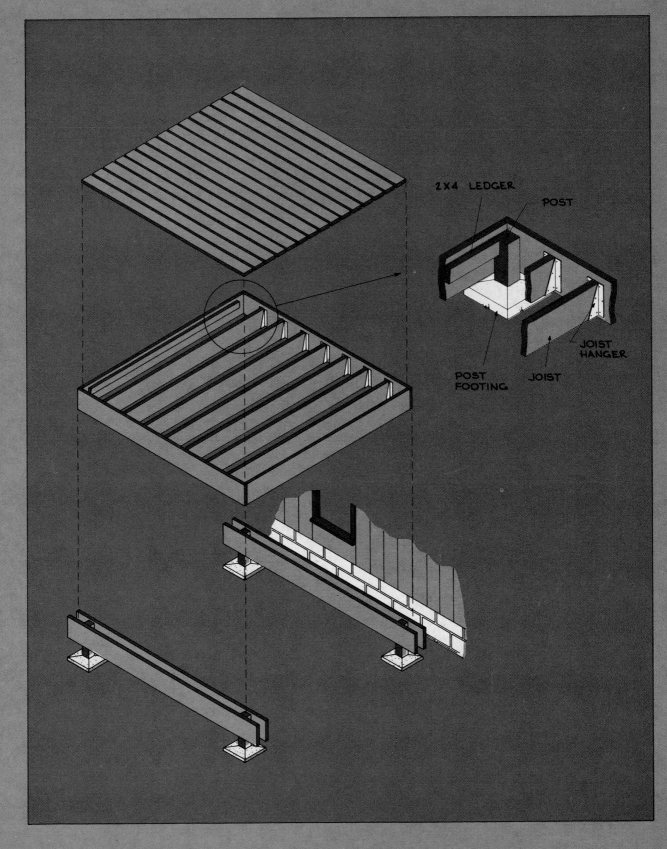

Bi-Level Deck

Here's a type that gives you the charm of two decks in one. The upper level provides a comfortable area near an entrance to your home, while the unenclosed lower level hugs the ground. Stairs between the two decks form a con-venient link, and can double for extra seating.

Constructing a bi-level deck amounts to building two separate decks . . . but the result is well worth your extra effort. Start by placing posts for both sections and attaching the beams to the posts. The upper level is an at-tached elevated deck, bolted to the header of the home, as the lower right cutout shows.

Next, construct the framing for both levels and mount it to the beams. Attach stair stringers and railings for the upper level and the stairs. Finally, lay the decking and stair treads.

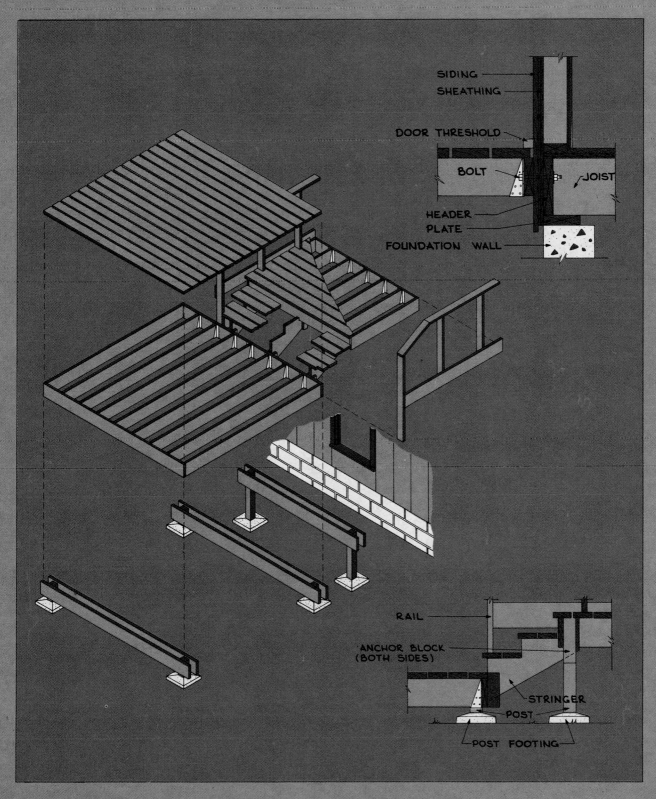

THE FINE ART OF LAYING DECK BOARDS

An art indeed! This part of your deck-raising lets you make your own personal statement. You can opt for one of the established patterns...or set the neighborhood on its ear with a floor that's as unique as your signature.

Design Possibilities

The sketches below depict four ways to make your deck unusual and interesting. Each of the designs takes a little extra time to create and requires a bit more material but the results are worth it.

You may even decide to design your own pattern. If you do, be sure to build in adequate support for all deck boards.

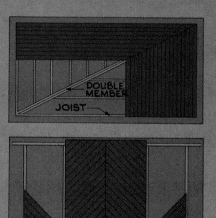

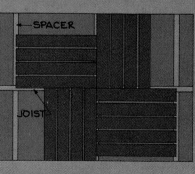

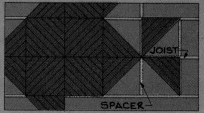

Nailing the Deck Surface

Lay boards bark side up to prevent cupping, and use 12d box nails or 16d galvanized casing nails for 2-inch decking. Drive two nails at each joist, leaving a ⅛- to ¼-inch space between boards so moisture will drain away and boards will dry off. For quick spacing, insert nails or plywood scraps as shown below.

When nailing into the ends of boards, drill slightly undersize pilot holes to prevent splitting. Before nailing dense or brittle wood that is likely to split, grind off nail tips. Blunt nails cut through the wood fibers; sharp ones wedge through wood, prying it apart.

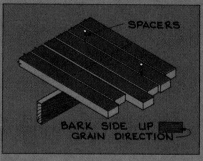

Make sure butt joints in deck boards meet on top of joists.

Measure As You Go

One difficulty you may experience while nailing down deck boards is keeping them parallel. To solve this problem, simply measure the distance remaining on the joists from time to time. Take measurements along both sides and the middle as shown in the sketch below. Tack a string line a foot or two away for a visual guide.

If, as you work, you discover that

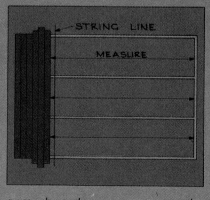

some boards are uneven, make your correction gradually, adjusting the space between the next

three or four boards.

When you have about 6 feet of decking left, begin adjusting board spacing to avoid an unsightly gap at the end of the deck.

Trim the Decking

For appearance's sake, you'll want to evenly cut off the exposed ends of deck boards. If you're skilled with a saw, you can snap a chalk line and cut boards off freehand. If you're not, tack a straight board in place as a guide for a

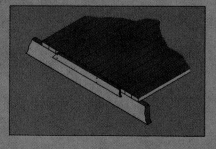

power saw, and keep the saw snug against the guide for a straight, smooth cut (see sketch). To eliminate sharp edges, bevel ends with a fine rasp or hand plane.

Skirt the Deck Boards

Another effective way to give the edges of your deck a finished look is to nail on a skirt of 1-inch lumber (see sketch). Do this as a finishing touch after attaching all railings, stairs, or other structures.

To avoid moisture buildup and subsequent rotting in skirting boards use rot-resistant redwood or cedar. If you use other types of wood, paint or treat them

with water-resistant stain before assembling.

You can achieve a similar finished appearance by recessing the deck's surface to the same level as the top edges of the headers and outside joists. The detailed drawing on page 52 shows you how.

STAIR BUILDING SIMPLIFIED

Most do-it-yourselfers view stair construction as one of the most mystifying portions of building a deck. But it doesn't have to be, as these instructions demonstrate. Start by thinking of stairs as a means of dividing a difference in elevation into a series of uniform steps to make it easy to get from one level to another.

Types of Stringers

The first thing to decide is which type of stringer, or step support, you'll use. You can use open stringers, which resemble the teeth of a saw, or opt for closed stringers that conceal the sup-

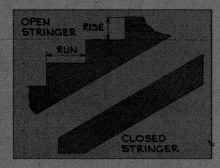

porting surfaces (see sketch above). Remember, *stringers are the most important parts of your stairs*. You must make them strong enough to carry heavy loads and be sure all of your cuts are made accurately for the sake of both safety and appearance.

Every stair step consists of a horizontal run and a vertical rise, as the sketch above shows. A rise of about 7 inches and a run of 10 or 11 inches is both comfortable and safe for most adults.

If you have a situation where a gentler incline would be attractive, use this rule: the sum of a run and rise is 18 inches. So, with a rise of, say, 4 inches, provide a 14-inch run. Keep in mind the importance of maintaining uniform rises and runs in each set of steps—unexpected changes can easily cause accidents.

To figure the number of steps a stair should have, first measure the total vertical distance between levels (labeled total rise in the

sketch below). Divide this by 7 inches or whatever rise you plan to use and round off the result to the nearest whole number (the number of steps). To calculate the exact rise per step, divide the total rise by this number.

Next, decide the length of run

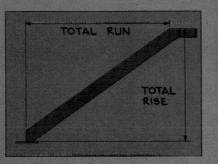

to use. Multiply that figure by the number of steps, and you have the total run of your stairs. Save these figures for laying out and notching or dadoing your stringers.

Ways of Supporting the Treads

Having determined the number of steps and the rise and run of each, you're ready to decide how you'll attach the stair treads—the surfaces of the steps. If you like the appearance of closed stringers —see sketch in next column— you can make them either by attaching cleats or making dado cuts to receive the treads. Using regular or extended cleats makes the job easier and also preserves the stringer's full strength.

The easiest way to make dado cuts is to use a circular handsaw with a dado set. Depth of dadoes should be ¼ to ⅓ of the stringer thickness.

Open stringers require a lot of accurate sawing—maybe more than you'll want to try without a power saw.

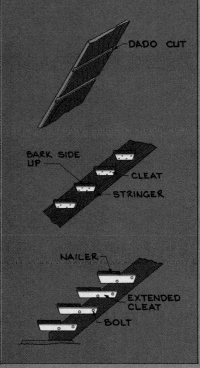

How to Lay Out and Cut Open Stringers

Proper layout is critical for open stringers. Using a framing square (see the sketch below), mark the run on the long side and the rise on the short side. Position the square so the edges of the square and the board meet at these marks. Then pencil in the rise and the run. Reposition the square so that the end of the next run intersects the end of the adjacent rise, and continue marking.

Runs as marked represent where the bottom of each tread will be. So, to keep all steps even, saw off the thickness of one tread from the bottom of the first rise.

For adequate strength in open stringers, 4 inches of knotfree wood should remain after cutting.

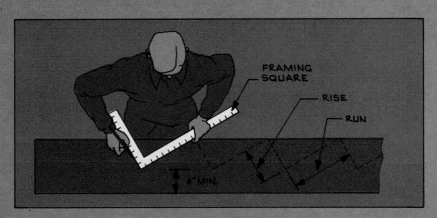

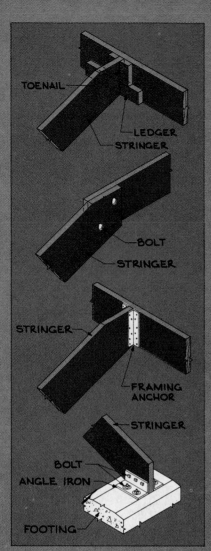

Securing the Stringers

For stairs to be safe, you must anchor them well. Basically, this means making solid joints between the stringers and frame.

As the sketch above shows, you have several choices in attaching the tops of stair stringers. The least complicated in terms of fasteners involves nailing up a ledger, notching the stringers to ride on the ledger, and toenailing the stringers in place. Finish by nailing blocks at the sides of the stringers.

Nearly as easy—and much stronger—is bolting the stringers to the ends of joists or headers. Using framing anchors as shown in the sketch also provides a good, strong attachment.

While the weight of a stairs usually is enough to hold the foot in place, you may want to attach the lower end to prevent possible shifting. The illustration shows a stringer foot bolted to a clip angle which, in turn, is bolted to a concrete footing.

With less effort, you can achieve nearly the same rigidity by setting in drift pins when you pour the concrete and positioning them so they extend into the base of the stringers.

Attaching the Treads

How you attach your stair treads depends partly on the material you decide to use. Your simplest choice is standard 2-inch lumber, as shown in the upper part of the sketch below. Be sure to lay treads "bark side up" to minimize warping (see sketch on page 54), and nail in place with 12d or 16d casing nails.

For closed stringers, drive two or three 16d nails through the stringer into the tread ends in the dado cuts. Or, if you use cleats, nail treads to them.

With open stringers, drive nails through the treads into the stringers, first drilling pilot holes to prevent splitting.

For massive good looks and even more character, consider building treads of 2x4s set on edge (see sketch); they're no more difficult to construct. Just make sure to separate 2x4s with ⅜-inch plywood spacers, nailing them together through the spacers. Attach them to cleats or extended cleat supports by toenailing, or with all-purpose framing anchors on the bottom of the treads.

You can also build treads of 2x4s on edge by nailing a frame-work in place as shown at bottom of page. Doing it this way eliminates the need for spacers.

Adding a Stair Rail

Stair rails perform the all-important function of safeguarding against accidents. So, even a short stair should have a rail 30 to 40 inches tall to provide adequate protection.

The key members of a stair rail are the posts. You may use balusters as shown in the sketch below, or simply elect to use one post at each end of the rail.

If you plan to use a 2x4 top rail, keep the span between posts under 6 feet. For 2x6 or larger rails, you can use spans of up to 8 feet. Attach the posts to stair stringers or deck framing with bolts or lag screws.

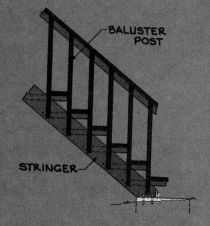

Your building code may spell out minimum requirements for your stair rails, But as long as it's safe and practical, try to style this stair rail after your deck railing.

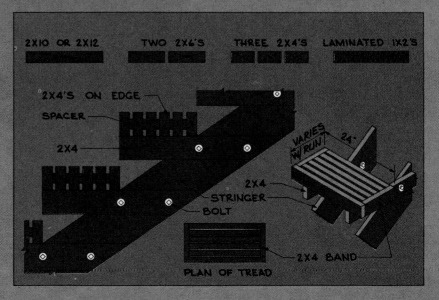

DECK RAILINGS FOR STYLE AND SAFETY

Granted, safety is the real reason for attaching a railing to an elevated deck. But there's no law that says it can't look good, too.

Popular Options

You can choose from many basic railing styles, as this sketch shows. An old standard is one built of 4x4 posts and 2x4 rails. Besides being economical, this

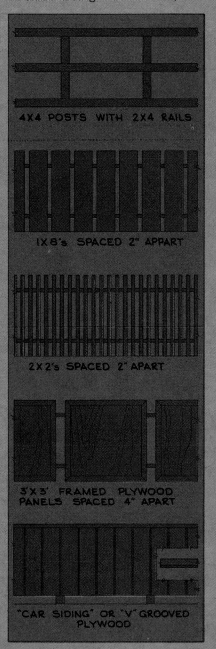

4X4 POSTS WITH 2X4 RAILS

1X8's SPACED 2" APPART

2X2's SPACED 2" APART

3'X3' FRAMED PLYWOOD PANELS SPACED 4" APART

"CAR SIDING" OR "V" GROOVED PLYWOOD

style features open construction that lets you take good advantage of a scenic view.

The next two railing styles are good-looking variations of a picket fence. Their framework consists of 2x4 or 4x4 posts spanned by horizontal 2x4 rails. To prevent these styles from sagging, keep spans under 6 feet. See pages 95-96 for details on joining posts and rails.

Using vertical boards evenly spaced—such as the 2x2s or 1x8s shown—gives you a railing that provides some privacy, yet permits free movement of air.

The trick to keeping pickets aligned is to hold a spacer in place while nailing up each one. To make sure they're vertical, check occasionally with a carpenter's level.

For still more privacy, use 2-foot-square panels spaced 4 inches apart, or consider car siding or grooved plywood panels. They enclose a railing completely, transforming it into a low wall open only at the bottom.

Attaching the Railing to the Deck

Often, you can use the posts that support the frame of the deck to

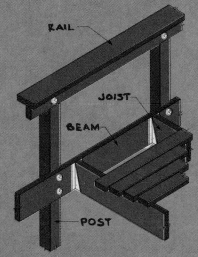

hold up the railing, too, as this drawing shows. Notice that the rail consists of a 2x4 bolted to the posts and capped with a 2x6. This cover protects the open grain of the post ends from moisture.

Another satisfactory method of attaching a railing is to bolt its posts to the header or outside joists of the deck. Secure them with 5/16- or 3/8-inch bolts through

the base of each post, as shown in sketch. To strengthen the joints,

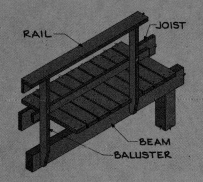

use washers on both sides, and galvanized bolts to resist rust.

One especially attractive way to attach a railing is with double posts, as shown below. Cut them

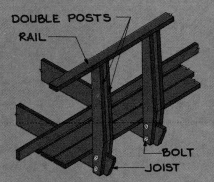

from 2-inch stock, bolt to both sides of extended joists, and attach rails as illustrated.

Another handsome alternative involves a combination of rails

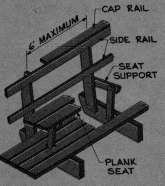

and seating as shown in this sketch. Slant seat back uprights outward slightly so that cap and side rails will provide a comfortable backrest.

For standard seating, build benches 15 to 18 inches high, with seats at least 15 inches wide. Backrests should extend at least 12 inches above the seats. You can use these bench-railing combinations on one or more sides of your deck.

COVERING YOUR DECK

A roof addition for your deck has to rank as one of the extras. But adding one, either now or later, could pay off handsomely in terms of livability. This is especially true if your deck needs shade or protection from the elements.

As with building the deck, planning ahead is a good idea here, too. So, keep the following points in mind:
• Check building codes to make sure your plans are acceptable.
• Make certain the structure is strong enough to support heavy weight, such as snow or a roofer.
• Make the topper sturdy enough to withstand high winds.
• Should you ever want to convert your covered deck into an enclosed porch, now is the time to provide adequate framing. Otherwise, remodeling will mean rebuilding.
• If the walls of your home enclose your deck on two or three sides, adding a roof without adequate ventilation could trap heat, turning your deck into an oven on hot days.
• If you're doubtful about the suitability of a roof for your deck, consulting an architect may save you expensive headaches.

Building a top for your deck is much like constructing the deck itself. Posts support both, and the covering is framed in much the same way as the deck's beams, joists, and headers. Attaching the roof frame to your home is also done similarly (see page 50).

The sketches on this page show covers designed for shade and privacy. The top cover features easy-to-make canvas panels that pull back to let in sun and sky. Insert 2x2 slats in sewed-in pockets, and attach the canvas at the rear of the frame.

In the middle sketch, a deck cover is constructed in the same way as the attached elevated deck on page 50. Here, decking boards provide plenty of shade and ventilation at the same time.

The bottom sketch is of a cover supported by posts on the outside and attached at the rear to the house. Diagonal decking boards and a skylight panel of ½-inch sheet acrylic dress up this topper.

HOW TO INSTALL A SLIDING GLASS DOOR

Easy access is essential if you want to use your deck for all it's worth. And there's no easier—or more impressive—transition from house to deck than a sliding glass door. And best of all, you can install one in a day.

What's Available

Sliding glass doors come in 6-, 8-, 9- and 12-foot widths, and require a rough opening a couple of inches larger than the unit size. The 6-footer is most popular and the least expensive.

Locating the Opening

In locating your new patio door, you have a couple of choices. You can enlarge an existing opening for a window or a hinged entrance door. Or you may decide to tear out a solid section of wall. But it's best to have the door on hand to make sure it fits your intended location before you begin work.

Once you've chosen a location, pencil the outline for the opening on the inside finished wall. Remove pictures and other wall hangings, move furniture away and turn back carpeting before cutting. Check, too, to see if electrical wiring will be disturbed by the opening. If so, turn off power before starting.

Opening the Inside Wall

With a hammer or hatchet, break through the wallboard or plaster to start your opening at about waist level. Making a horizontal cut a few inches high along the full width of your rough opening will help you locate all the studs that will be affected.

After locating the studs, remove the rest of the inside wall cover. The opening should extend on one end the distance of one stud further than the rough opening you'll need. Use a keyhole saw or saber saw along the outside studs to make clean cuts in the wallboard or in the plaster and lath.

Before cutting away any of the studs, brace the ceiling joists a

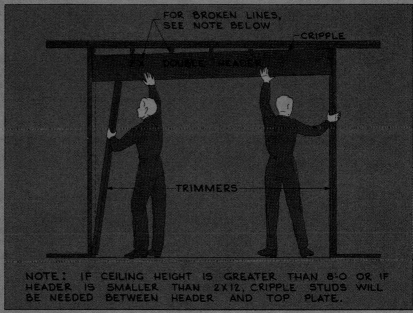

NOTE: IF CEILING HEIGHT IS GREATER THAN 8'-0 OR IF HEADER IS SMALLER THAN 2x12, CRIPPLE STUDS WILL BE NEEDED BETWEEN HEADER AND TOP PLATE.

few feet in from the wall. Lay a 2x8 or larger plank on the floor and hold another against the ceiling, parallel to the wall. Then wedge several 2x4 uprights snugly in place to provide support.

Next, prepare the header for insertion into the opening. (For a 6-foot door, use a pair of 2x8 headers on edge; for an 8-footer, two 2x10s; and for a 9- or 12-foot door, two 2x12 headers.) To do this, nail the 2-inch material together with a ½-inch spacer in the middle. Measure length, and cut for a close fit between studs.

Depending on the depth of your header, you may need cripple studs to close the rough opening to the correct height (see sketch above). If so, mark and saw them off accordingly. Pry the lower end of each cut stud away from the sheathing and siding and pull it out of wall. If you don't need cripple studs, cut through existing studs and remove pieces.

Installing the Header

Butt one end of the header against an existing stud and insert the trimmer as illustrated. Repeat this operation at the other end of the header. If necessary, install double trimmers under the header to adjust the rough opening to the correct width. Using 16d common nails, nail the trimmers and studs together. Toenail the header and trimmers at each end of the opening with 8d common nails. With header now in place, you can remove the tem-

porary ceiling support.

Cutting the Opening

In each of the upper corners, drill holes through the sheathing and the siding, then start cuts along the studs with a keyhole saw. Continue cutting with a handsaw until you cut through the base plate (see sketch below). Remove the base plate, drill holes in the lower corners, and finish the opening by making horizontal cuts along the bottom of the header and flush with the floor's surface.

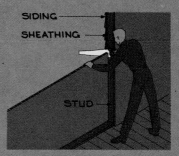

You must make one modification in the rough opening before installing the door: remove an inch or so of siding at the sides and top of the opening so the door molding will fit tightly against the sheathing and the siding will butt against the edge of the molding. Measure carefully and pencil straight lines to be cut. Set your circular saw depth to cut through the siding only and make your cuts.

Complete the installation, following the instructions packed with your siding door.

A PATIO SAMPLER

A patio can be as nondescript as a small concrete slab adjacent to your house, or as elaborate as some of the stately ones shown in this chapter. But plain or fancy, there's no quicker way to add outdoor living space to your home than with a patio.

And it's not that difficult, either. Just study the examples in this chapter and read the material in the Patio Building Basics section that follows, and you shouldn't have any problems laying any patio you choose.

As far as design goes, you're in the driver's seat. Make your patio any size and shape that's complementary with your house. And choose from stone, concrete, brick, tile, and even wood to use singly or in combination for striking results.

STONE: IT'S RUGGEDLY HANDSOME

Where appearance is paramount, stone is perhaps your wisest surfacing choice. Its rugged natural texture yields visual character that few other surfaces can match.

Not surprisingly, stone is also the most expensive patio surfacing option. But once in place, it's maintenance free.

Depending on the look you want, there's a type of stone to suit your exact needs. Flagstone, either as uncut rubble or in random-sized rectangles, is available in a variety of rich, earthy colors—buff, yellow, reddish brown, and gray.

For a slightly different yet equally attractive look, consider bluestone or slate in deep shades of blue, green, gray, and red.

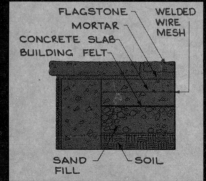

1 Select a patio design and site (see page 70).
2 Excavate site (see page 71).
3 Spread and level a 4-inch layer of sand or fine gravel.
4 Top sand or gravel with 15-pound building felt.
5 Cover the felt with wire mesh.
6 Pour a 4-inch layer of concrete and let cure for a couple of days (see pages 72-73).
7 Embed 1½- to 2-inch-thick stones in about ¾ inch of mortar, allowing a ½-inch space between stones (see page 74).
8 Tap stones till level and smooth up joints with a trowel.

BRICK: WITH AN AIR OF ELEGANCE

Brick adds a note of distinction and permanence to your home and patio, and it does this at relatively little expense. With 10,000 different color, texture, and size combinations available, your choices are practically limitless. And once you decide which one is right for you, there are literally several dozen different pattern possibilities for laying it (page 74 shows several arrangements).

You can lay brick on a bed of sand and use sand joints brushed into the cracks, or lay it in mortar on top of concrete. Either method provides a durable, carefree surface.

Note: Always use SW (Severe Weather)-grade brick.

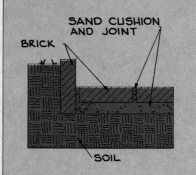

1 Develop your plan before starting construction (for ideas, see page 70).
2 Excavate to the depth needed to accommodate thickness of patio surface and underlayment (see page 71). Make sure edges of excavation are vertical and smooth.
3 Set edging brick on end along the perimeter, as illustrated.
4 Spread and level a 1½-inch cushion of sand (see page 74).
5 Lay brick flat in selected pattern, leaving a ½-inch space for joints on all sides.
6 Sweep loose sand over brick until joints are filled, removing any excess when finished.

CONCRETE: PRACTICAL FLEXIBILITY

With concrete, you can be as creative as you wish. You can pour it into almost any shape, and finish it with a variety of surfaces. Try stamping or scoring geometric patterns for unusual effects... or expose aggregates on the surface... or add a pigment to the mix.

But there's nothing wrong with a smooth or slightly skid-resistant concrete surface, either. It can be exceedingly attractive, especially when accented with a low brick wall as shown here.

Although only moderately expensive, concrete is extremely durable. And even if you've never worked with it before, you'll find pouring and finishing is easy, too.

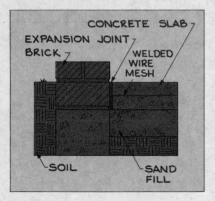

1 Plan your project beforehand then double-check your plan by laying it out (see pages 70-71).

2 Remove sod and excavate deep enough for thickness of supporting fill and slab (see page 71).

3 Pour footing for edge of patio. Let cure for a day.

4 Spread 4 inches of sand fill and level (see page 71).

5 Position ½x4-inch expansion joint material along the inside of the brick edging (see sketch).

6 Pour concrete slab, finish, and let cure (see pages 72-73).

7 Backfill outside of edging and add plantings.

CONCRETE SLABS: EASY GOOD LOOKS

Why are concrete patio blocks so very popular? Because they're attractive and convenient to use: you buy them ready to lay.

These blocks usually are 2 inches thick and are available in a variety of sizes and shapes, including a Spanish tile pattern.

If you want concrete slabs larger than are commercially available, you can make them yourself. Simply construct forms for units 2 or 3 inches thick and as large as you want (and can move). Then pour and finish the concrete, and place when cured.

You can lay patio blocks on a bed of sand, fine gravel, or packed soil with equally good results. Simply fill the joints with sand or soil.

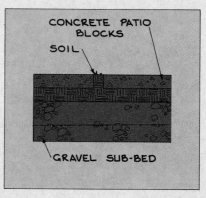

CONCRETE PATIO BLOCKS

SOIL

GRAVEL SUB-BED

1 Consider how you will use your patio as you make plans to build it (see page 70).

2 Remove 10 inches of soil.

3 Spread 6 inches of fine gravel or sand on bottom of the excavation (see page 74). Check grade to make sure moisture will drain off finished surface.

4 Spread a 2-inch layer of soil on top of gravel, as shown.

5 Lay patio blocks on top of the soil, making sure each one is level with adjacent blocks.

6 Fill 1- to 2-inch-wide joints with soil and sweep clean.

CLAY TILE: TO STATE FORMALITY

As a patio surface, clay tiles have a lot going for them. They're smooth-looking, resistant to wear from heavy foot traffic, and easy to clean. And last but not least, the orderly patterns in which you can lay tiles give a tile patio a gracious, formal look.

Tile is available in several sizes, colors, and shapes. Two types are manufactured: quarry tile and patio tile. The former is smooth and regular, while patio tile may have an uneven, handcrafted look. Although both are expensive, they provide a smashingly good-looking surface.

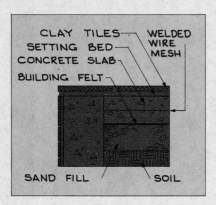

1 Draw up a workable set of plans (see page 70).
2 Dig site about 9 inches lower than the level of the finished surface—deeper around the perimeter (see page 71).
3 Spread a 4-inch bed of sand and level it within the patio perimeter (see page 74).
4 Cover with 15-pound building felt, as illustrated.
5 Pour concrete slab on top and allow to cure for at least one week (see pages 72-73).
6 Lay tile in ¾-inch bed of mortar and work mortar into the seams to serve as grout.

PATIO BUILDING BASICS

You've seen some terrific patio ideas on the preceding pages and by now have a good notion of what you want. Now it's time to jump in and build your own.

If the thought of being ankle-deep in a sea of sloppy cement makes you cringe, don't worry.

Patio construction is simple. You won't need many tools. And if you don't have those needed, you can rent them.

From planning the job to finishing the surface to edging your patio, it's all simply explained in this helpful section.

WORKING UP A PLAN

As with all major home improvement projects, you should always start by checking your zoning ordinances and building codes (see page 45). Within these guidelines, you're free to plan and build as you wish, but you should keep these points in mind.

Site. Climate, more than any other single factor, will determine how much you use your patio. Luckily, you can plan around the climate to a certain degree. See page 45 for details.

Consider, too, the normal flow of human traffic, and position your patio so that it's easy to reach, but still private enough to ensure your comfort.

Terrain also will influence your site selection. If the ground next to your house falls away steeply

or climbs sharply, you may have to bring in fill dirt or excavate.

Size and shape. The size patio you decide on is entirely up to you, but one helpful rule of thumb is to plan an area that is approximately equal to the largest room in your home.

As for shape, squares and rectangles are easiest to construct, but you can build free forms tailored to the terrain, shrubbery, or yard structures with only a minimum amount of extra effort.

LAYING OUT THE PATIO

Once you have a particular size and shape in mind, make a sketch of your plan. Be sure to draw in the patio accessories and furniture you'll be using, too. Then, with sketch in hand, go to the site and double-check how well your plan will work.

One clever way to visualize a free-form patio in your chosen location is to roll out a garden hose along the perimeter. If the curves just don't seem to work, change them till they do.

When you're satisfied with the outline, mark it with stakes at regular intervals.

Establish the Perimeters

For a rectangular patio, start by measuring off the length adjacent to the house and driving stakes at each corner. From these stakes, measure the width of the patio in lines perpendicular to the wall of the house. Drive stakes at the outside corners just deep enough to

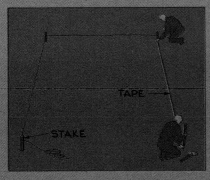

hold. Check to make sure they are square, using the 3-4-5 method described on page 48.

Then, drive stakes in securely and encircle them with a chalk line or string to establish the patio's perimeter (see sketch).

Excavate the Area

The finished surface of your patio should be even with the ground or an inch or so above it. To accommodate the thickness of the surface and the base, you'll need to excavate between 5 and 6 inches of soil from the area.

Start by stripping away the existing sod as illustrated. With an old butcher knife, a spade, or a shovel, make parallel cuts 2 or 3 inches deep and 1 foot apart. Intersect these with perpendicular cuts every 3 feet. These cuts will make it easier to lift pieces of sod. Or, you may want to consider renting a sod cutter.

Set Up Forms

Use straight, knot-free 2x4s held in place with 1x2 or 1x4 stakes 18 to 24 inches long. Start by driving corner stakes at one end of the patio. Temporarily nail the form to the stake near the house and level it. Before nailing both ends securely in place, adjust to allow a slope, away from the house, of ⅛ to ¼ inch per foot of form length. Being careful to keep the form aligned, drive stakes every 3 feet, all flush with or just below the top of the form.

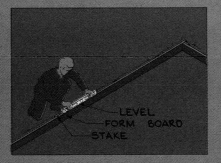

Next, put up the other end form, parallel to the first one and with an identical slope. Add the remaining sides, using butt joints at the corners and driving 7d or 8d common nails through the forms into the stakes (see sketch above).

How to Form Other Shapes

You can make gradual or relatively sharp curves in the edge of your concrete patio by building the appropriate forms as shown

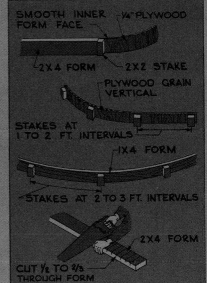

here. For short-radius curves, cut 3½-inch-wide strips of ¼-inch plywood so grain runs vertically.

For gentle curves, you can spring 1x4s into place and nail them to the stakes. By sawing "kerfing" cuts an inch or so apart and ½ to ⅔ through 2x4s, you can make them pliable enough to form curves. Bend toward the cut side to close the kerfs. Be sure to stake curved forms every 1 to 3 feet, using more stakes on the thinner forming material.

Prepare the Base

A 2-inch-deep layer of fine gravel or sand provides a sound base for a concrete patio. Spread it with a shovel until it looks level. Then, with a 1-inch-thick board cut to the right length, strike off the surface of the base so it's level with the bottom of the form.

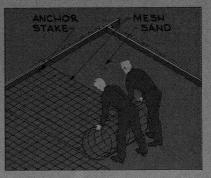

Next, to add strength to the concrete slab, roll out, cut to fit, and stake in place 6x6-inch mesh made of no. 10 wire, as shown in the sketch above.

POURING THE CONCRETE

Once your forms are up and the base is ready, obtain the tools you'll need to handle and finish the concrete. These include a straight 2x6 a foot or two longer than the width of your patio, to use as a screed, a bull float, a wood float (also called a darby), a flat steel trowel, a pointed mason's trowel, an edger, and a jointer.

Line up several strong, healthy helpers and at least two heavy-duty wheelbarrows if you can't pour directly into the forms.

Estimating needs. There are a couple of different ways to do this. Either consult the chart on page 87 or use this guide: a 100-square-foot slab 4 inches thick requires 1.23 cubic yards of concrete. The same 100 square feet 5 inches thick takes 1.54 cubic yards. When figuring your needs, be certain to allow an extra 10 percent for waste.

How to mix your own. Dry pre-mixed concrete is available in bags. But it's expensive, so use it only for small jobs.

It's better to do your own mixing, using a ratio of 3 parts aggregate (gravel), 2 parts sand, and 1 part dry cement. Mix in water to a mushy consistency in a tub.

When to order ready-mix. For jobs exceeding 1 cubic yard, consider ordering wet ready-mixed concrete (see page 87 for more information). And if you have had no experience pouring and finishing concrete, limit your order to 3 cubic yards.

Ready, set, pour! Just before pouring concrete, wet the ground and forms with a fine spray from a hose.

Start your pour at one end, spreading the mushy concrete with a shovel as illustrated at top of next column, and work toward the other end. As much as possible, dump the concrete in its final position, placing each succeeding load against the previous one and filling forms full or slightly heaped in the middle.

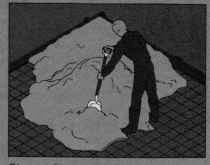

Shovel-fill any low areas and run a trowel around the edges to fill gaps.

With a hook, pull up on the wire mesh to embed it in the wet concrete (see sketch below).

FINISHING THE CONCRETE

Start this operation after only a fraction of your cement is poured. There's a good reason for doing it this way: If there's too much cement in one part of the form, it can be moved easily into the unfilled area. If too little, simply pour in some more.

Screeding

To bring the soft concrete to its final level, strike it off with a screed board as illustrated at top of next column. Move it in a sawing motion while pulling it forward, pressing down on forms.

If cement piles more than 2 or 3 inches high in front of the screed, move the excess away with a shovel. If low spots appear, shovel them full, move the screed back, and strike off again. Two or three passes with the screed will ensure a level job.

Bull Floating

Immediately after striking off the wet cement, begin bull floating (see sketch below). This levels ripples left by screeding and settles the aggregate below surface.

Immediately after you finish bull floating, be sure to cut the concrete away from the form to a depth of 1 inch with the tip of a pointed trowel.

Edging and Jointing

When the water sheen is gone and the concrete has stiffened slightly, do the preliminary edging with a ½-inch-radius edger, working along the form as illustrated in the sketch below. Put in

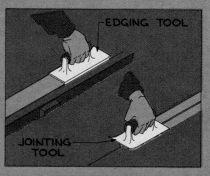

joints with a jointer (see sketch). Do the final edging and jointing just before you begin the brooming operation.

Troweling

When the concrete will support you so your feet sink less than ¼ inch, it's time to start your finishing operation. For a relatively even but rough texture, use a wood hand float in a swirling pattern. With a 2x3-foot piece of plywood for a kneeboard, work the hand float in wide, sweeping areas, as the sketch below shows, backing away as you work.

For a smooth surface, use a steel trowel when the concrete is quite stiff. Little or no cement should cling to the trowel as you work, and it should make a ringing noise as you smooth the slab. Wash your trowels with water as soon as you're through working with them.

Brooming

For a skid-resistant texture without float marks, draw a damp broom over the surface. Do this when the concrete is hard enough to retain the grooves or marks made by the broom. You can control the roughness of the texture to a great extent by using a soft- or stiff-bristled broom.

As the previous sketch shows, a broom can produce an amazing variety of surface patterns.

Curing

To make your concrete strong and durable, you must cure it properly. This means keeping it continuously wet for at least 5 days in warm weather (70 degrees F. or

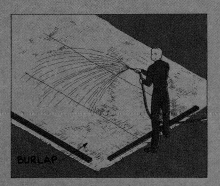
BURLAP

higher) and for 7 days at milder temperatures. Cover the concrete with burlap and keep it soaked as illustrated above. Or keep a plastic sheet in place over the slab to prevent excessive drying.

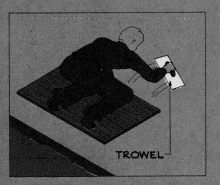

TROWEL

SPECIAL-EFFECT SURFACES

The sky's the limit when it comes to designing a surface to suit your own taste (see sketch).

For instance, you can embed exposed aggregate by scattering pebbles on the concrete surface right after bull floating. When concrete has stiffened some, trowel and sprinkle on a retarder. Hose clean after concrete sets up.

Or, you can press geometric designs into the surface while it's soft. Trowel, dress grooves, and broom slightly to finish.

Other possibilities include applying the swirl design, wavy broom pattern, or circle design when surface is ready to finish.

For the keystone finish, broom a coarse texture into the surface, then spatter on ridges of soft mortar made of pigmented white cement and sand (mixed 1:2), leaving patches of rough surface exposed. As the mortar hardens, trowel smooth.

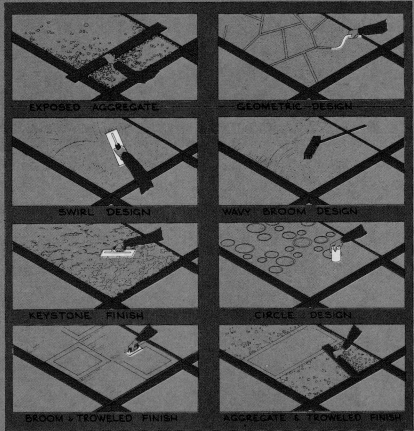
EXPOSED AGGREGATE | GEOMETRIC DESIGN
SWIRL DESIGN | WAVY BROOM DESIGN
KEYSTONE FINISH | CIRCLE DESIGN
BROOM & TROWELED FINISH | AGGREGATE & TROWELED FINISH

OTHER PATIO SURFACES

If you've been racking your brain over something to make your patio a real standout, take a good look at these alternative surfacing materials: brick, flagstone, or patio blocks.

You can lay them in a million different patterns (well, almost!) that will set your patio apart from all the rest. Either lay these materials in mortar on top of concrete slabs or bypass pouring cement and put them on a base of fine gravel or sand.

Preparing the Base

Stake out your site as discussed on pages 70 and 71. Then remove sod and excavate to a depth of 4 or 5 inches overall, and 6 to 8 inches along the sides. With a spade, form a smooth vertical wall to back the outside course of your surface material.

Before laying any material in place, spread a base of sand ½ to 1 inch deep. If your patio is next to your house, this base should slope away at ⅛ to ¼ inch per foot. For patios in level areas away from other structures, slope the surface in all directions from the middle. A sand leveling board made from 1x4s or 1x6s makes this job easier (see sketch).

Once the sand is in place, soaking it with a coarse spray of water will settle it. After firming, go over the surface again, smoothing it overall. To stop weed growth, put down 15-pound building felt.

Setting the Surface Material

After choosing your surface material, select a pattern for laying it out. Below are several alternatives for setting brick.

Allow a ⅛- to ¼-inch space between brick joints, and about ½ inch between flagstone pieces. Using the butt of a hammer handle, tap the surface material into level position so all edges are even (see sketch at top of next column).

It's helpful to make a dry run, putting part of the bricks or stone

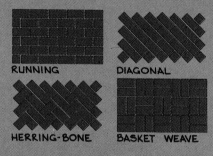

RUNNING   DIAGONAL

HERRING-BONE   BASKET WEAVE

in place to see how they'll look. At this point, you can easily rearrange them if necessary. Once they meet your approval, set the remaining surface material in place.

Finishing the Surface

The easiest way to complete a brick, stone, or patio block surface is to sprinkle sand over the area and sweep it back and forth until it fills the joints. Then sweep up excess. The result is a pleasingly solid surface.

For joints that stop weeds and grass from popping up and that resist moisture, which can freeze and wreck a patio surface, consider using cement. Mix 1 part of

portland cement to 3 parts sand, and sprinkle the dry mix over the patio surface, sweeping it back and forth until the joint spaces are full (see sketch above). Clean up the excess.

Next, wet down with a fine spray as illustrated, being careful

not to wash the mortar mix from the joints. Repeat spraying the surface two or three more times at 15-minute intervals to make sure that the mortar is wet throughout. It will then harden within a few hours and cure within a week.

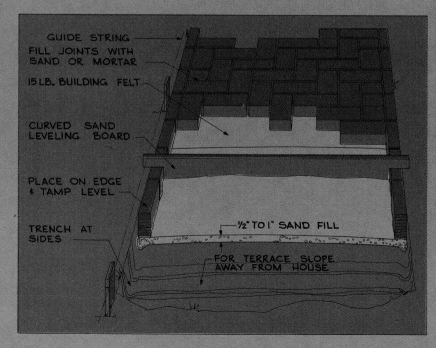

GUIDE STRING
FILL JOINTS WITH SAND OR MORTAR
15 LB. BUILDING FELT
CURVED SAND LEVELING BOARD
PLACE ON EDGE & TAMP LEVEL
TRENCH AT SIDES
½" TO 1" SAND FILL
FOR TERRACE SLOPE AWAY FROM HOUSE

EDGING — THE FINAL TOUCH

Nothing sets off a patio better than a distinctive edging. Shown are some popular treatments.

For example, a course of brick around the perimeter of a concrete patio adds tasteful contrast. Or, you might consider a low brick wall along one or more patio sides for a pleasing effect.

Conversely, an edging of simple concrete will nicely frame a patio with an intricate brick pattern. For a really unusual treatment, mix a powdered pigment into the concrete before pouring the edging. Use either complementary or contrasting colors.

Another attractive idea is to place loose materials in a trench around the edge of a patio. The key to a successful treatment is to erect metal edge strips along the perimeter to maintain clean, straight lines. It's also a good idea to line the trench bottom with a strip of black plastic film or building felt to retard the growth of weeds and grass.

Between the edge strip and the patio surface, you can pour bark or wood chips for a touch of the forest. Or, elect the earthy looks of pea gravel or pebbles. Crushed rock—especially white marble—adds an eye-catching accent.

Also, consider the ever-popular railroad ties for a patio edging. There are good reasons for their being such favorites: besides having a rugged appearance, they're treated to resist rotting, making them a durable choice for patio edging and even steps embedded in the soil.

If you've anything of a green thumb, ground covers or other plantings are a natural edging choice. Ground huggers such as sedum or periwinkle, or low shrubs such as pfitzer juniper are good selections. On the other hand, you may wish to consider arranging flowers in beds or portable pots to add a welcome splash of color to your patio scene.

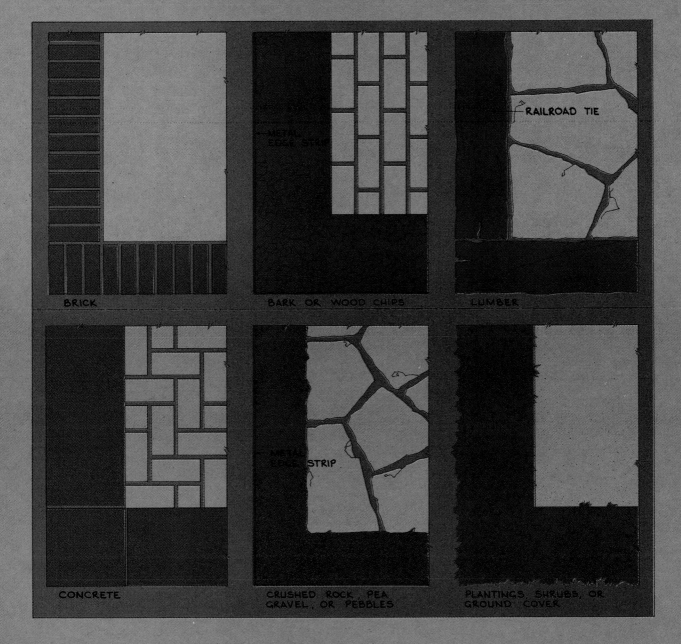

BRICK

BARK OR WOOD CHIPS — METAL EDGE STRIP

LUMBER — RAILROAD TIE

CONCRETE

CRUSHED ROCK, PEA GRAVEL, OR PEBBLES — METAL EDGE STRIP

PLANTINGS, SHRUBS, OR GROUND COVER

DECK AND PATIO DRESS-UPS

Now that you've built the deck or patio of your dreams, why not outfit your outdoor oasis with custom-made furniture? It's easy, inexpensive, and something you'll enjoy doing in your spare time.

You'll find you don't have to be an experienced furniture craftsman to build the professional-looking projects in this chapter. All of these ideas use simple construction techniques and easy-to-accomplish woodworking skills. Just select a project that appeals to you (modifying the dimensions, if necessary, to fit your special needs), choose your materials, and follow the step-by-step instructions.

The result? A beautiful new planter for your patio. Or a great-looking bench and table ensemble for your deck. There are many projects to choose from on the following pages . . . but if you're adventuresome, don't stop there. Go ahead and be your own furniture designer, using the projects presented here as idea starters. Perhaps you have a few scraps of lumber left over from building your new deck or patio. If so, put them to use . . . and enjoy!

FREE-SWINGING PATIO GLIDER

Take a minute to look over the drawing and step-by-step instructions for this exciting project—the construction is surprisingly simple! You'll see that the seat of this graceful glider swings back and forth on metal straps bolted to a sturdy, stationary base. Tough polyurethane varnish protects the glider against heat, cold, and moisture... and glossy black enamel paint adds a stylish accent to the metal hardware.

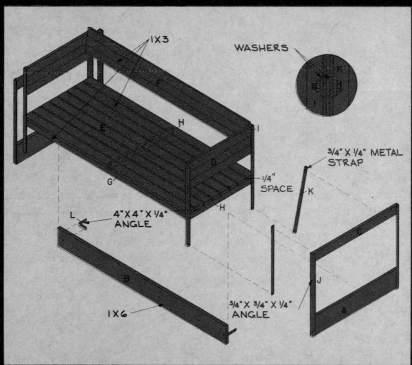

1 To build the stationary base, cut lengths of 1x6 (A) and 1x3 (C) for sides. Cut metal angles (J) to size. Drill holes and bolt sides together.

2 Bolt 1x6 stretcher (B) to sides, using angle braces as shown.

3 Next, assemble bench-like glider. Cut 1x3 slats (D) for arms; bolt to metal angles (I).

4 Construct a frame for the glider seat from 1x3s (G, H), butting together with glue and nails. Glue and nail on 1x3 seat planks (E).

5 Drill holes and screw arm assemblies to glider seat.

6 Cut three lengths of 1x3 (F) to form seat back. Screw to arms.

7 Drill holes in sides of base (C) and in iron straps (K) for hanging glider bench assembly. With help, lift glider to proper height and attach iron straps to glider and base. Use washer assembly as shown (see sketch detail).

8 Varnish and paint.

Materials (for a 30x60-in. glider):
1x6 pine—10 ft.
    A 2 30 in.   B 1 58½ in.
1x3 pine—92 ft.
    C 2 30 in.
    D 6 22 in.
  E,G 10 57 in.
    F 3 55½ in.
    H 3 20½ in.
¾x¾-in. metal angle—16 ft.
   I,J 8 24 in.
¾-in. metal strap—7 ft.
    K 4 20 in.
Angle braces, glue, nails, screws, lag bolts, varnish, paint.

MOSAIC DECK OR PATIO TABLE

This fashionable table gets its inlaid appearance from geometric patterns of varnished redwood strips. If you want, you can build matching benches, too. Just use construction techniques similar to the ones given for the table.

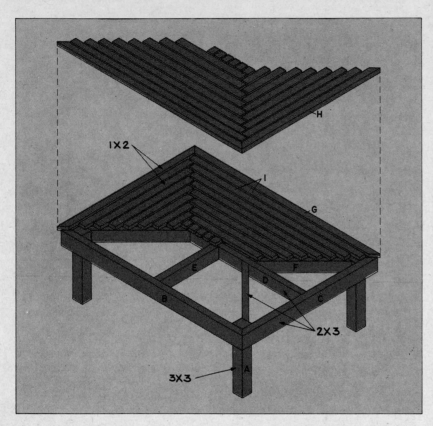

1 Glue and nail mitered 2x3s (B,C) to form tabletop frame.
2 Cut 3x3 uprights (A) to size. Screw one upright into each corner of frame, countersinking screwheads and plugging holes.
3 Install 2x3 stretcher (D) inside frame; strengthen with 2x3 cross-members (E,F), mitering corners as necessary.
4 For tabletop, miter corners on 1x2s (G,H) to form outer frame. Cut 1x2 slats (I) to size. Before installation, stain (if desired) and varnish.
5 Install tabletop, starting with outer 1x2s and working toward center. Glue and nail slats to base, spacing ¼ inch apart. Countersink nailheads, fill holes.

Materials (for a 36x47½x16¾-in. table):

3x3 redwood—6 ft.

A	4	16 in.		

2x3 redwood—28 ft.

B	2	46½ in.	C	2	35 in.
D	1	43½ in.	E	2	15¼ in.
F	4	20⅛ in.			

1x2 redwood—86 ft.

G	2	47½ in.	H	2	36 in.
I	2	44 in.	I	2	40½ in.
I	2	37 in.	I	2	33½ in.
I	2	30 in.	I	2	26½ in.
I	2	23 in.	I	2	19½ in.
I	2	29 in.	I	2	25½ in.
I	2	22 in.	I	2	18½ in.
I	2	15 in.	I	2	11½ in.
I	2	8 in.	I	11	4½ in.

Wood plugs, glue, screws, nails, wood putty, stain (if desired), varnish.

FLIP-TOP DECK MATE

The beauty of this combination privacy screen/storage bench is its versatility. It's great as a comfortable seat to escape the hot summer sun. And, you can store your barbecue gear and charcoal beneath the handy flip-up bench top.

1 Build box-like bench by gluing and nailing sides (B,C), bottom (E), and divider (D) together.

2 Butt together 1x4 frame (H,I) for privacy screen. Glue and nail back set of stops (J) to frame.

3 Nail lattice strips (K) to stops, spacing ½ inch apart. Leave gap in center for 1x4 support (M). Add a second set of stops (J) at top.

4 Paint screen and bench.

5 Set bench on penta-treated 1x4s (L) laid flat underneath.

6 Fit bench within 1x4 screen frame; nail into place.

7 Cut top sections (F,G) for bench. Paint. When dry, join together with three butt hinges. Notch corners to fit around screen frame and attach to bench.

8 Face bench with lattice (A).

9 Attach 1x4 center support (M) as shown with glue and nails.

Materials (for a 32½x72-in. unit):

¾-in. plywood—2½ shts.
E 1 69x29½ in. F 1 71x12 in.
B 2 69x16½ in.
C 2 31x16½ in.
D 1 29½x15¾ in.
G 1 71x19¼ in.

1x4 pine—42 ft.
H 2 72 in.   I,L 4 70½ in.
M 1 53¼ in.

1x1 redwood—18 ft.
J 6 34⅞ in.

¼x1½-in. lattice—315 ft.
K 36 70½ in.   A 66 16½ in.

Glue, three butt hinges, penta, and paint or stain.

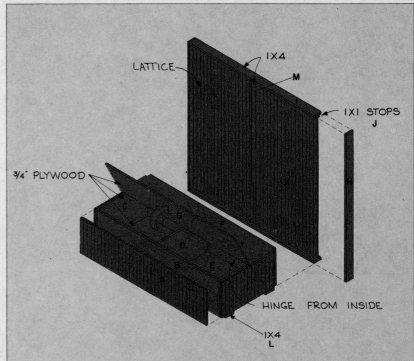

LATTICE — 1X4 — M

¾" PLYWOOD

1X1 STOPS J

HINGE FROM INSIDE

1X4 L

REDWOOD PATIO BENCH

Whether surrounded by flower gardens or parked at poolside, this sturdy bench is an ideal addition to any patio. Build several to take care of a crowd! For a permanently placed bench, bolt it right into the patio surface or use longer legs and set in concrete.

1 Build leg assemblies first. Cut 4x4 uprights (A) to size; then, cap each upright with a 1½-inch piece of 3x3 (B) as shown.

2 Cut two 4x4 horizontal support beams (C). Drill holes and double-bolt leg assemblies together, running long bolts completely through uprights and horizontal beam (be careful to position horizontal beams at proper height).

3 For seat supports, cut four identical lengths of 2x6. Rip one inch off the width of two of the boards to form supports (E). Cut a 1-inch-deep notch along the length of supports (D) as shown. Screw and glue all four seat supports onto leg assemblies.

4 Build a frame for seat top from mitered 2x3s (F,G). Glue and nail together. Attach frame to seat supports; then, glue and nail 2x3 seat slats (H) into place, spacing slightly apart.

5 If desired, stain and varnish.

Materials (for a 60x24x18-in. bench):

4x4 redwood—14 ft.
   A 8 14 in.   C 2 24 in.
3x3 redwood—2 ft.
   B 8 1½ in.
2x6 redwood—24 ft.
D,E 4 60 in.
2x3 redwood—72 ft.
   F 2 52¼ in.   G 2 24 in.
   H 28 21 in.

Nuts and bolts, glue, stain, and varnish (optional).

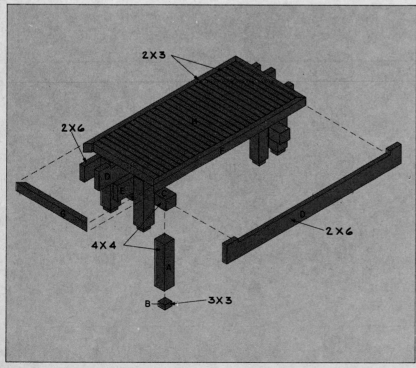

WRAPAROUND REDWOOD SEATING

Landscaping your deck or patio is great fun . . . and once you've planted some beautiful trees and shrubs, you'll want to protect them from wayward feet. A wraparound bench arrangement like the one shown here is a good way to prevent guests and family from accidentally treading on your ground-level plantings. And as a bonus, you'll benefit from some comfortable, naturally shaded seating, too!

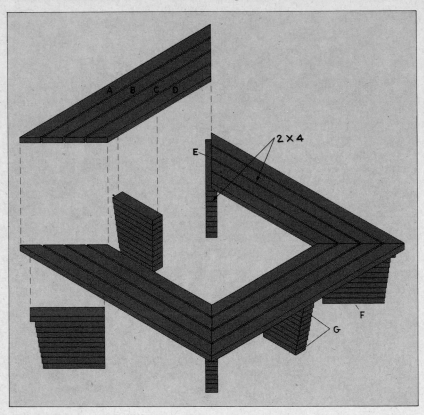

1 Build legs for bench from 2x4 scraps or lengths of lumber cut to size. For each leg assembly (F,G), stack up pieces of 2x4 (F) one on top of the other, increasing length of each 2x4 by ¼ inch as you stack them. Glue and nail together as you go. At each corner, use longer 2x4s (E) for support.

2 Cut 2x4 planks (A,B,C,D) for bench seat, mitering corners as shown. Glue and nail to legs, spacing each plank ¼ inch from the next.

3 If desired, stain bench or treat with weathering oil.

Materials (for a 16½-in.-high, 14¾-in.-wide bench):

2x4 redwood—164 ft.

A	4 65½ in.	B	4 58 in.
C	4 50½ in.	D	4 43 in.
E	6 17⅜ in.		

F 4 corner legs, each containing 9 2x4s, the shortest being 13 inches, the others increasing by ¼ inch to 15 inches.

G 2 center legs, each containing 9 2x4s, the shortest being 11½ inches, the others increasing by ¼ inch to 13½ inches.

Nails, exterior glue, and stain or weathering oil.

CONTOUR DECK BENCH

Construct this bench as a "built-in," dramatically sweeping up from the horizontal lines of your existing deck. Or, use the idea to build a freestanding bench for any type of deck or patio surface. Either way, this versatile project works like a charm!

1 *For a built-in bench,* cut out an 11½-inch section from decking for each bench leg. If no joists run beneath, install at least two to support the bench.

2 Cut out bench legs (A) in shape shown (adjust curve in legs according to space between joists and deck surface). Install legs, anchoring to joists with long screws or nails.

3 To build bench seat assembly, construct a frame of 2x4s (C, D), mitering corners and gluing and nailing together. Fill in the frame with 2x4s (B) set on edge and spaced ¼ inch apart.

4 Attach bench seat assembly to legs with angle braces or dowels.

5 Stain or treat the bench with weathering oil.

6 *For a freestanding bench,* construct as above using shorter legs (see materials list). Using a threaded rod, bolt a 2x4 spacer (E) between each leg.

Materials (for a 53½x19½-in. freestanding or built-in bench):

2x12 redwood—20 or 26 ft.
  A 15 16 in. (freestanding)
  A 15 19½ in. (built-in)
2x4 redwood—48 or 62 ft.
  B 7 50½ in.   C 2 53½ in.
  D 2 15½ in.
  E 14 11½ in. spacers
     (for freestanding bench)
Angle braces or dowels, threaded rods, glue, and stain or weathering oil.

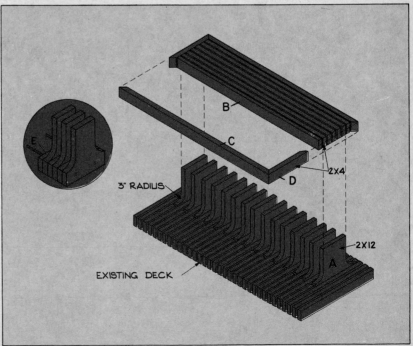

B

C

D

2x4

3" RADIUS

E

EXISTING DECK

A

2x12

TREE-SIZE PLANTER

Building a deck or patio doesn't necessarily mean sacrificing your favorite green growing things. Instead, transplant them into an assortment of planters and built-in gardens —the more the better! For dramatic landscaping, construct a jumbo planter like the one shown here.

1 Cut out hexagonal planter bottom (F). Butt 1x4s (A) to bottom at corners, mitering edges to fit. Nail and glue each corner assembly together.

2 Cut 2x4 top plates (B), mitering corners to fit shape. Nail to previously assembled corner uprights. Follow by nailing on remaining 1x4 slats (A) between corners, spacing ¼ inch apart.

3 Face outside bottom of planter with mitered 1x3s (C).

4 Treat interior wood surfaces with wood preservative. Allow to dry for two or three days.

5 Line inside of planter walls and bottom with sheet metal (E), overlapping seams (drill holes in bottom for drainage). Nail pentatreated 1x3s (D) around inside top edge of planter, mitering corners.

6 If desired, stain or treat with weathering oil.

Materials (for a 20-in.-high planter):

¾-in. plywood—½ sht.
   F 1 34x34 in.
2x4 redwood—12 ft.
   B 6 $20\frac{9}{16}$ in.
1x4 redwood—48 ft.
   A 30 18½ in.
1x3 redwood—20 ft.
   C 6 $19\frac{1}{16}$ in.
   D 6 18 to 18½ in.
28-gauge galvanized sheet metal
   E 1 54x54 in. sht.
Glue and stain or weathering oil.

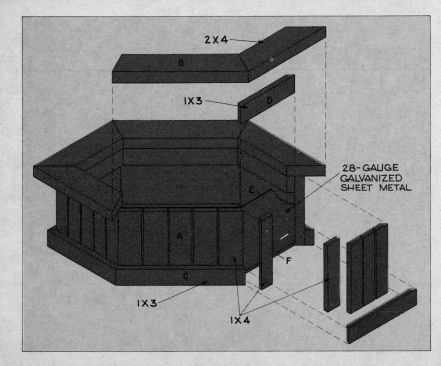

BREEZY PRIVACY FENCE

Want to build a privacy fence without closing off those pleasant, fresh air breezes? Here's a clever solution! Build this fence from redwood, then stain it an earthy color to keep the natural look. Remember ... check local building codes before getting started.

1 Purchase 4x4 fence posts (A) long enough to extend below frost line. Stain all fence boards and posts before construction.

2 Treat bottoms of posts with penta preservative and allow to dry for two or three days.

3 Determine locations for posts and dig holes. Set posts into holes anchoring with concrete. Check to be sure posts are straight before concrete hardens (see instructions on pages 94-95).

4 Nail on 2x6 top plate (D). Follow with 1x6 fence boards (B,C), spacing slightly and allowing room for 1x1 trim strips (F). Nail trim strips into position.

5 Finish lattice-type section of fence by nailing 1x1 strips (E) into place. Add vertical 1x1 trim (H) as shown.

6 Finish fence by nailing on vertical 1x2 trim (G).

Materials (for a 13-ft.-long, 76-in.-tall fence section):

4x4 redwood—48 ft.
   A 4 12 ft.
2x6 redwood—14 ft.
   D 1 13 ft.
1x6 redwood—88 ft.
   B 8 96 in.   C 2 12 ft.
1x2 redwood—24 ft.
   G 4 64½ in.
1x1 redwood—218 ft.
   E 40 48 in.   F 4 12 ft.
   H 2 56½ in.
Cement, penta, stain, and nails.

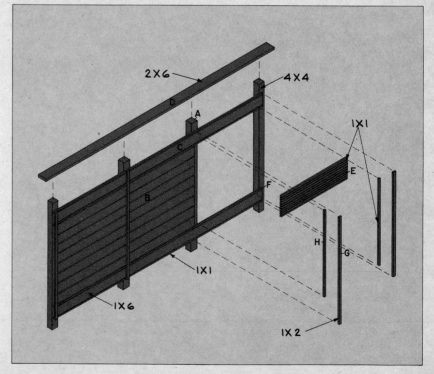

PLANNING/ BUILDING BASICS

Having attractive, well-built accouterments for your deck or patio is easy, especially if you take the time to learn the basics.

OUTDOOR PROJECT POINTERS

Let's face it! Projects you keep outside will have it pretty rough. You can make things easier, though, by first realizing this, then doing something about it. Consider these tips:

Furniture

Traditionally, redwood, cypress, and cedar have been used for garden and patio furniture. However, the weather-resistant qualities of even these excellent woods will leach out after a few years and they'll become weatherbeaten. What to do?

One easy solution is to apply a stain that will still allow the grain to show, but a better bet is two coats of exterior enamel paint. Thin the first coat with turps—if it's an alkyd paint—and apply the second coat without thinning.

Construction. Needless to say, you should always use waterproof glue in the construction of outdoor furniture. If the patio chairs and chaises are to be left in their natural state—unpainted—it's best to use galvanized or aluminum nails, or brass screws for fastening. However, if you plan to paint you can use steel nails, screws, and bolts.

When building a patio table or bench, allow for drainage. A good way to do this is to space the boards 3/8 inch apart.

Rot. A potential weak point in all outdoor furniture is the legs. Because they're constantly immersed in water after a rainfall and during snowstorms, legs draw moisture into the end grain. A simple remedy for this is to install plastic glides to cover the bottom of each leg.

Lighting

Good outdoor lighting will greatly increase the time that you can enjoy your backyard and garden. But, be sure to observe the following rules: If the power line is to be buried underground, make sure that it's the kind approved for burial. It should have a grounding wire, and all outlets to the line should be of the grounding type. And also make sure that any tools or appliances you use outdoors have a three-prong plug that automatically grounds them.

Low-voltage lighting. To avoid any possibility of shock hazard, consider low-voltage lighting, which operates safely on 24 volts supplied by a transformer.

Ground fault interrupter. This device turns off the electric current within 1/50 second after you touch an appliance that has become "shocking."

Concrete Work

Wait for good weather before starting your project. However, if you start a job and the temperature drops to freezing despite what the weatherman said, protect the newly laid concrete from freezing by covering it with burlap, rags, and newspapers. The same procedure applies during extremely hot weather.

Concrete less than an inch thick has little strength. But you can use a thin layer to repair chipped steps or sidewalks if you first apply a bonding agent to the existing concrete.

Use the chart shown here to figure out how much concrete you will need for a given job. For a small job, you can buy dry ready-mixed concrete in bags; all you need do is add water.

If you need more than one cubic yard, consider purchasing wet ready-mixed concrete. This will arrive at the pouring site in a truck and will be dumped where you indicate. So make sure the forms are ready when the truck arrives (most concrete companies charge extra if you make them wait). It's best to have a neighbor or friend on hand to help you with the job, too.

When setting a fence post into concrete, make sure that the bottom of the post does not project beyond the concrete into the earth. The concrete should be below the frost line and at least four inches above grade. Slope it away from the post for drainage purposes, and use black asphalt roofing cement to seal junctures where post and concrete meet. Fence posts should be 4x4s—nothing lighter.

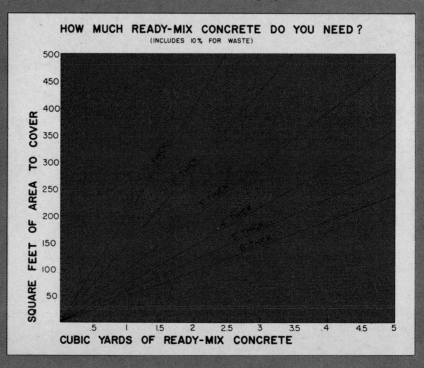

HOW MUCH READY-MIX CONCRETE DO YOU NEED?
(INCLUDES 10% FOR WASTE)

SQUARE FEET OF AREA TO COVER

CUBIC YARDS OF READY-MIX CONCRETE

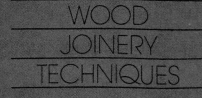

WOOD JOINERY TECHNIQUES

No matter what material you're planning to use, it will have to be cut to size—measure twice and cut once is a good rule—then put together using glue, nails or screws, and one of these joints.

Butt Joints

The simplest joint of all, the butt joint, consists of two pieces of wood meeting at a right angle and

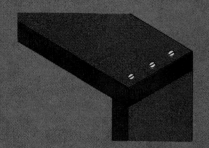

held together with nails, or preferably, screws (see sketch). A dab of glue before using the nails or screws will make the joint even more secure. But don't use glue if you're planning to take the work apart sometime later.

When reinforced by one of the six methods illustrated, the butt joint is effective for making corner

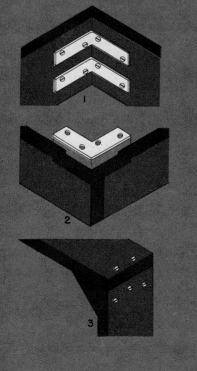

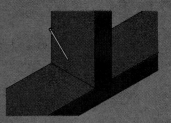

joints. Two common fasteners are corner braces (1), and flat corner plates (2). Using scrap wood, you can reinforce the joint with a triangular wedge (3), or with a square block (4). A variation of the square block places the block on the outside of the joint (5). Finally, a triangular gusset made from plywood or hardboard will also serve to reinforce a corner butt joint (6).

When a butt joint is in the form of a T—for example, in making a framework for light plywood or hardboard—you can reinforce it with a corner brace, T plate, or corrugated fasteners.

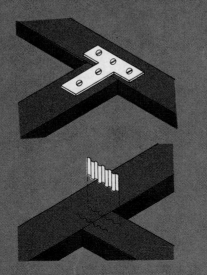

For really rough work, you can drive in a couple of nails at an angle, or toenail (see sketch). A variation of this is to place a block of wood alongside the crosspiece

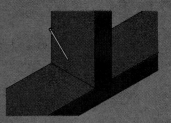

and secure it with a couple of nails.

A close cousin to the T joint and the butt joint is the plain overlap joint. It is held in place with at least two screws (see sketch). For extra reinforcement, apply glue between the pieces of wood.

Butt joints are an excellent means of securing backs to various units, especially when appearance is not a factor. Simply cut the back to the outside di-

mensions of the work, then nail in place . . . it's called a flush back.

Lap Joints

On those projects where appearance is vital, consider full and half-lap joints. To make a full lap joint, cut a recess in one of the pieces of wood equal in depth to the thickness of the crossmember (see sketch).

The half-lap joint is similar to the full lap joint when finished, but the technique is different. First, cut a recess equal to half the

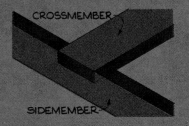

CROSSMEMBER

SIDEMEMBER

thickness of the crossmember halfway through the crossrail. Then, make a similar cut in the opposite half of the other piece (see sketch on the next page).

Butt joints and overlap joints do

not require any extra work besides cutting the pieces to size. However, full and half-lap joints

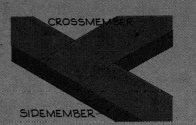

require the use of a backsaw and a chisel. For a full-lap joint, mark off the thickness and width of the crossmember on the work in which it is to fit.

Use the backsaw to make a cut at each end that's equal to the thickness of the crossmember, then use a chisel to remove the wood between the backsaw cuts. Check for sufficient depth and finish off with a fine rasp or sandpaper. Apply white glue to the mating surfaces and insert two screws to hold the joint securely.

Dado Joints

The dado joint is a simple way of suspending a shelf from its side supports. To make a dado joint, draw two parallel lines with a knife

across the face of the work equal to the thickness of the wood it is to engage (see sketch). The depth should be about one-third of the thickness of the wood.

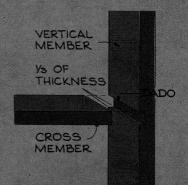

Next, make cuts on these lines and one or more between the lines

with a backsaw. Then, chisel out the wood to the correct depth.

You can speed the job immeasurably by using a router, a bench saw, or a radial arm saw. Any one of these power tools makes the cutting of dadoes an easy job — and provides much greater accuracy than can be achieved by hand.

If appearance is a factor, consider the stopped dado joint. In this type of joint, the dado (the cutaway part) extends only part way, and only a part of the shelf is cut away to match the non-cut part of the dado.

To make a stopped dado, first make your guide marks and chisel away a small area at the stopped end to allow for saw movement. Then make saw cuts

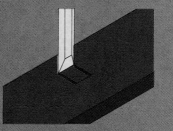

along your guide marks to the proper depth. Next chisel out the waste wood as shown in sketch.

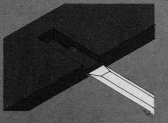

And finally, cut away a corner of the connecting board to accommodate the stopped dado.

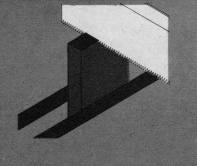

Rabbet Joints

The rabbet joint is really a partial dado. As you can see in the drawing at the top of the following column, only one of the meet-

ing members is cut away.

The rabbet joint is a simple one to construct, and it's quite strong, too. To ensure adequate strength, be sure to secure the meeting members with nails or screws and glue.

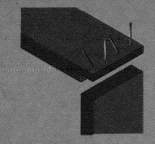

This joint is often used in the construction of inset backs for units such as cabinets and bookshelves (see the sketch below). To make this joint, rabbet each of the framing members, then care-

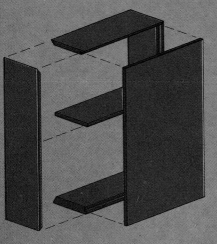

fully measure the distance between the rabbeted openings. Cut the back accordingly. Then use thin screws to secure the back to the unit.

Mortise and Tenon Joints

A particularly strong joint, the mortise and tenon joint is excellent when used for making T joints, right-angle joints, and for joints in the middle of rails. As its name indicates, this joint has two

parts—the *mortise*, which is the open part of the joint, and the *tenon*, the part that fits into the mortise.

Make the mortise first, as it is much easier to fit the tenon to the mortise than the other way around. Divide the rail (the part to be mortised) into thirds and carefully mark off the depth and the width of the opening with a sharp pencil.

Next, use a chisel, equal to the width of the mortise, to remove the wood between the pencil marks. You can expedite this job by drilling a series of holes in the rail with an electric drill, a drill press, or even a hand drill. (If you have a drill press, you can purchase a special mortising bit that will drill square holes, believe it or not.) Mark the drill bit with a bit of tape to indicate the desired depth. Now use the chisel to remove the excess wood.

To make the tenon, divide the rail into thirds, mark the required depth, and use a backsaw to remove unwanted wood. If you have a bench or radial saw, the job of removing the wood will be much easier. Use a dado blade and set the blades high enough to remove the outer third of the wood. Reverse the work and remove the lower third, leaving the inner third intact.

To assemble, make a trial fit, and if all is well, apply some white glue to the tenon and insert it into the mortise. If by chance the tenon is too small for the mortise, simply insert hardwood wedges at top and bottom.

Use moderate clamping pressure on the joint until the glue dries overnight. Too much pressure will squeeze out the glue, actually weakening the joint.

Miter Joints

You can join two pieces of wood meeting at a right angle rather elegantly with a miter joint. And it's not a difficult joint to make. All you need is a miter box and a backsaw, or a power saw that you can adjust to cut at a 45 degree angle.

Since the simple miter joint is a surface joint with no shoulders for support, you must reinforce it. The easiest way to do this is with nails and glue (see sketch at the top of the following column). You'll notice that most picture

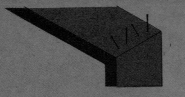

frames are made this way.

However, for cabinet and furniture work, you may use other means of reinforcement. One way is to use a hardwood spline as shown in the drawing. Apply glue to the spline and to the mitered

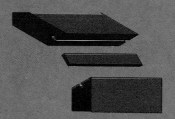

area and clamp as shown until the glue dries.

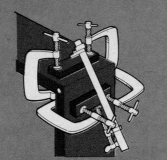

A variation of the long spline uses several short splines—at least three—inserted at opposing angles.

Dowels are a popular method of reinforcing a mitered joint, too. Careful drilling of the holes is necessary to make certain the dowel holes align. Use dowels that are slightly shorter than the holes they are to enter to allow for glue at the bottom. Score or roughen the

dowels to give the glue a better surface for a strong bond.

Dovetail Joints

The dovetail joint is a sign of good craftsmanship. It's a strong joint especially good for work subject

to heavy loads.

To make the joint, first draw the outline of the pin as shown and

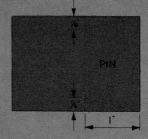

cut away the excess wood with a sharp backsaw. Place the pin over the second piece of wood and draw its outline with a sharp pencil. Make the two side cuts with the backsaw and an additional cut or two to facilitate the next step—chiseling away the excess wood. Then test for fit, apply glue and clamp the pieces until

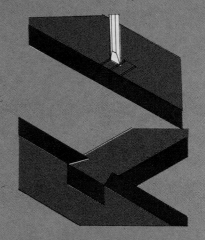

dry. This is the basic way to make most dovetail joints. However, it's much easier to make dovetail joints with a router and dovetail template, especially made for home craftsman use.

Corner Joints

These joints are used for attaching legs to corners for framing. A good technique for joining corners is the three-way joint involving a set of steel braces you can buy. First, insert the bolt into the inside corner of the leg. Then cut slots into the side members, and secure the brace with two screws at each end. Finally, tighten the wing nut.

A variation of the three-way joint uses dowels and a triangular ¾-inch-thick gusset plate for additional reinforcement. To make this joint, first glue the dowels in

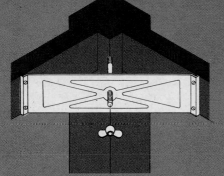

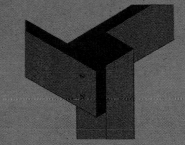

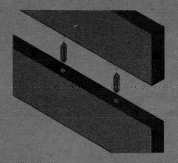

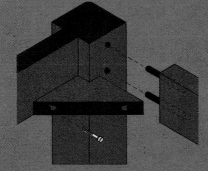

the vertical piece (see sketch). Let them dry completely, then finish the assembly.

A glued miter joint, reinforced with screws and glue, also makes a good corner joint. Make sure the screws do not penetrate the outside surface of the mitered joint.

Probably the strongest of the corner joints is the mortise and tenon (with mitered ends) reinforced with screws (see sketch). The miters on the ends of the tenons allow for a buildup of glue in the mortise, which in turn makes the joint stronger. Make sure that the holes you drill for the screws are not in line with each other.

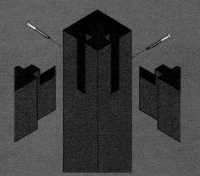

Otherwise, the wood may split. Use flathead screws and countersink the holes.

The simplest corner joint of all is a butt joint for the two horizontal members (see sketch). Instead

of being fastened to each other, the butted members are each fastened to the corner post with screws.

Edge-to-Edge Joints

Whenever an extra-wide surface is required, such as a desk top, workbench, or a large storage cabinet, this joint fills the bill. To make it, glue together two or more boards, then hold securely with either bar or pipe clamps. If the boards have a pronounced grain, reverse them side-to-side

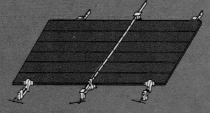

to minimize warping. For additional strength, screw cleats to the underside of the boards.

You also can use hardwood splines to join several boards. Cut a groove the exact width of the spline along the meeting sides of the two boards (see sketch). Cut the grooves slightly deeper than the spline width and in the exact center of the board thickness. The best way to cut such grooves is with a router or a bench saw.

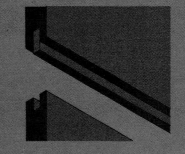

Then assemble with glue and clamps.

Another possibility for joining several boards involves the use of dowels. To make this joint, first

make holes in the boards. You can either use a doweling jig or a drill. If you use a drill, first drive brads (small finishing nails) into one board and press them against the second board to leave marks for drilling. Make the dowel holes slightly deeper than the dowels. Score the dowels, apply glue, join the two boards together, and clamp with pipe or bar clamps until the glue sets (allow plenty of time).

If you'll be drilling many dowel holes, you may want to use a wood or metal template to ensure accurate spacing.

Box Joints

One joint is so common in the construction of boxes — and drawers — it's called a box joint, or a finger joint because its parts look like the outstretched fingers of a hand (see sketch). Note that one of the mating pieces must have two end fingers, or one more

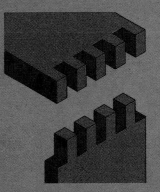

finger than the piece it is to engage. You can make this joint by hand with a backsaw and a small, sharp chisel. However, it is much easier, quicker, and more accurate to make it on a bench saw. Use a dado blade set to the desired width and proper depth of the fingers and mark off the waste area so there will be no mistake as to what you want to cut away.

THE HARDWARE YOU'LL NEED

For any sort of fastening work, you will need nails, screws, and bolts, as well as glues and cements.

Nails, Screws, and Bolts

These most common of all fastening materials are available in diverse widths and lengths, and in steel, brass, aluminum, copper, and even stainless steel.

Nails. Nails are sold by the penny—which has nothing to do with their cost. The "penny," (abbreviated *d*) refers to the size. The chart shows a box nail marked in the penny size designations as well as actual lengths in inches.

BOX NAIL
PENNY SIZE

d	in.
2	1"
3	1 1/4"
4	1 1/2"
6	2"
8	2 1/2"
10	3"
12	3 1/4"
16	3 1/2"
20	4"

Use common and box nails for general-purpose work; finish and casing nails for trim or cabinetwork; and brads for attaching molding to walls and furniture.

COMMON SCREWS

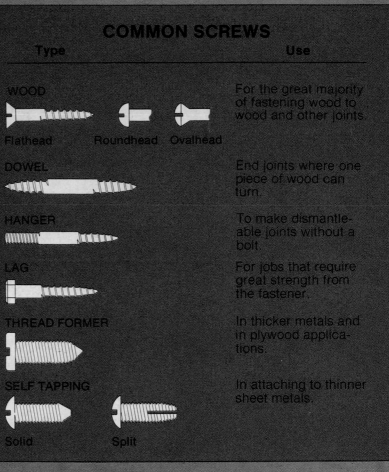

Type	Use
WOOD — Flathead, Roundhead, Ovalhead	For the great majority of fastening wood to wood and other joints.
DOWEL	End joints where one piece of wood can turn.
HANGER	To make dismantleable joints without a bolt.
LAG	For jobs that require great strength from the fastener.
THREAD FORMER	In thicker metals and in plywood applications.
SELF TAPPING — Solid, Split	In attaching to thinner sheet metals.

Finishing

Casing

Brad

Screws. Screws are sold by length and diameter. The diameter is indicated by a number, from 1 to 16. The thicker the screw shank, the larger the number. The drawing shows some of the most popular types of screws.

Always drill a pilot hole when inserting a screw into hardwood. And always drill a clearance hole in the leading piece of wood when screwing two pieces of wood together. Without a clearance hole, the leading piece tends to "hang up," preventing a tight fit between the two.

Bolts. You can also fasten wood together with bolts, but only if there is access to the back for the required washer and nut. A bolted joint is stronger than a screwed joint, as the bolt diameter is generally thicker than the comparable screw, and also because the wrench used to tighten the nut can apply much more force than a screwdriver in a screw slot.

Glues and Cements

While not "hardware" as such, glue is an important adjunct to any fastening job. The so-called white glue is excellent for use with wood, and only moderate clamping pressure is required. When dry, it is crystal clear. However, it's not waterproof so don't use it for work subject to excessive dampness—and of course, never for outdoor use. Use the two-tube epoxy "glue" for joints that must be waterproof.

Plastic resin glue, a powder that you mix with water to a creamy consistency, is highly water resistant.

Contact cement provides an excellent bond between wood and wood, and wood and plastic. When working with contact cement, remember that it dries instantly, so position your surfaces

COMMON BOLTS

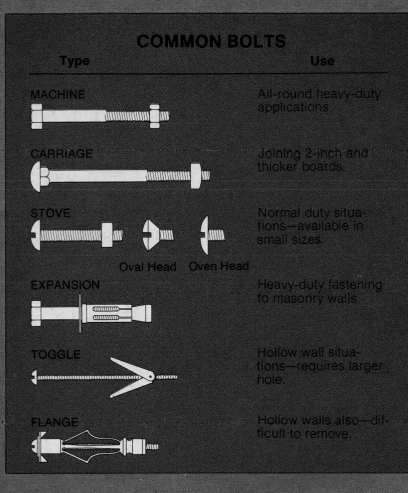

Type	Use
MACHINE	All-round heavy-duty applications.
CARRIAGE	Joining 2-inch and thicker boards.
STOVE — Oval Head, Oven Head	Normal duty situations—available in small sizes.
EXPANSION	Heavy-duty fastening to masonry walls.
TOGGLE	Hollow wall situations—requires larger hole.
FLANGE	Hollow walls also—difficult to remove.

When to Use What Glue

Type	Use
White glue (No mixing)	Paper, cloth, wood
Epoxy (requires mixing)	Wood, metal, stone (waterproof)
Plastic resin (requires mixing)	Wood to wood (water resistant)
Contact cement (no mixing)	Wood to wood or plastic (waterproof)
Waterproof glue (requires mixing)	Wood to wood (waterproof)

together exactly as you want them. You won't get a second chance.

True waterproof glue comes in two containers; one holds a liquid resin, the other a powder catalyst. When dry, this glue is absolutely waterproof and can be safely used for garden equipment and all outdoor projects and furniture.

Glides and Casters

The intended use determines whether a piece of furniture needs a caster or a glide. If you don't plan to move it frequently, use a glide; otherwise, a caster is the best choice.

Glides come in many sizes, determined by the glide area touching the floor, and with steel or plastic bottoms. The simple nail-on glides aren't height adjustable but you can adjust screw glides by screwing the glide in or out to prevent wobbling if the floor is uneven, or if by some chance, the project does not have an even base.

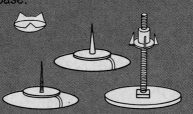

Casters are made in two styles—stem type (only the stem type is adjustable) and plate type (at left in sketch). The stem type requires a hole to be drilled into the leg or base of the cabinet or furniture. This hole accepts a sleeve that in turn accepts the stem of the caster.

The plate type caster is merely screwed to the bottom by four screws that pass through holes in the plate. They are not height adjustable unless, of course, you use shims.

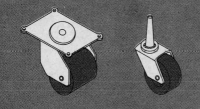

All casters use ball bearings as part of the plate assembly to facilitate swiveling. For extra-heavy usages, purchase casters with ball-bearing wheels as well.

The wheels on casters are of two types—plastic or rubber. Use casters with plastic wheels if the project is to be rolled on a soft surface such as a rug; rubber wheeled casters are best on hard concrete, vinyl, or hardwood. It's a good idea to use graphite to lubricate the wheels and their bearings, as oil tends to pick up dust and dirt.

To prevent a caster-equipped unit from rolling, get locking casters. A small lever on the outside of the wheel locks a "brake." Brakes on only two of the four casters on a unit are sufficient.

Miscellaneous Hardware

There are many types of hardware that can come in handy when you're constructing storage bins, cabinets, chests, shelves, and other projects.

Following are some you may need from time to time: corrugated fasteners connect two boards or mend splits in wood; angle irons reinforce corners; flat and T plates also reinforce work; masonry nails secure work to concrete or brick walls; steel plates with a threaded center are used for attaching legs to cabinets; screw eyes and cup hooks allow for hanging items inside storage units; and lag screw plugs made of lead or plastic secure furring strips or shelf brackets to masonry walls.

You'll be wise to stock your workshop with most of these items in a couple of sizes. That way, you won't have to make a special trip when they're needed.

HOW TO BUILD A FENCE

There's nothing like a fence to proclaim, "This is my little corner of the world." And, if built with a little care, a fence will serve you well for years.

Planning the Job

Whether built for privacy or for protection, a fence can become an integral part of your home's landscape. So, you should plan accordingly.

A privacy fence should be high enough to prevent passersby from looking into your grounds and windows. A fence built for protection should be strong enough to prevent animals from entering the grounds and to keep youngsters confined to the yard. It may not stop human intruders, but at least it will discourage them.

The first thing you need to do after you've decided to build a fence is to check the boundary lines of your property to avoid encroachment on your neighbor's lot. Professional fence installers often recommend building a fence six inches within your property lines to avoid possible hassles due to a faulty survey.

You'll need 4x4-inch posts at each end, at each side of any gates, and at intermediate intervals every six feet. For lightweight fencing, such as latticework, intermediate posts set every eight feet will suffice.

Redwood and cedar are traditionally used for fence posts because of their excellent resistance to rot and weather. However, you can use other wood provided you treat it with "penta" (pentachlorophenol), a chemical solution applied by generous brushing or dipping.

A creosote application below ground level and painting above ground level also will help to preserve the posts. Some lumberyards can supply pretreated lumber on order.

After determining how much lumber you need, arrange for the delivery of the posts—and if possible, for the fencing a few days later. If you set the posts in concrete, which is advisable, allow a few days to elapse—even a week—before starting the actual installation of the fence.

Inasmuch as lumber is commonly sold in 12-, 14-, and 16-foot lengths, plan to set the posts at 6-, 7-, or 8- foot intervals. By doing this you can cut in half the lumber that you buy for the horizontal part of the fence without any waste.

Setting the Posts

Having established the boundary lines of your property, drive a stake at each end, tie a heavy cord between the stakes, and draw it tight. Next, measure off the post intervals—and a gate, if required—and drive in stakes to indicate where you're going to dig the postholes.

If the soil is fairly free of rocks, use a posthole auger. This is like an oversized carpenter's auger with an eight-inch span; a smaller size with a six-inch span also is available. Use the smaller size only if the post is not to be set in concrete. Dig the hole deep enough to avoid heaving due to frost. (Frost lines vary all over the country, so be sure to check with a builder or architect to find out how deep it is in your area.)

If the soil is rocky, you'll have to resort to a clamshell posthole digger (see sketch). If you encounter large rocks, you don't need to move to a new location. A crowbar, sledge, and cold chisel will help.

But if the rock turns out to be as big as a house, don't try to dig it out. Instead, use a star drill and a sledge to drill a hole in the rock to a depth of five inches or so. Fill the hole with concrete (sand and cement, no stones) and force a 12-inch-long steel rod into the concrete-filled hole. Leave it and continue with the rest of the postholes. After the concrete has set, it's safe to install the post at this problem spot. Drill a slightly undersize hole in the bottom of the post and drive it onto the rod.

You can set posts directly into the holes if you first treat them with a penta solution or creosote to prevent rot. Generously brush either solution over the post, or better yet, make a trough in which you can immerse the posts overnight (this procedure ensures sufficient coverage). If you use a brush, pay particular attention to the bottoms of the posts, as this is where water can do the greatest damage.

There are four methods of setting posts. You can set and hold them in place by tamping the soil firmly around the post; by nailing cleats across the below-ground parts of the post; by pouring a collar of concrete around the post and shaping it to drain off water; or by setting the post into concrete.

For light-duty fences, if the soil is sufficiently firm and the hole you have dug has about the same diameter as the post, it's safe to use the first method. Fill the bottom of the hole with coarse gravel or small rocks to a depth of two inches for drainage. Next, set your post. Fill the hole part way with earth, tamp it down firmly, and continue filling and tamping.

Cleats nailed across the post will, of course, require a considerably wider hole, but you can employ the same tamping and filling procedure.

If you decide to use the third method, form a slight depression around the post and pour concrete around it. When the concrete has started to set, shape it so it will shed water.

The last method—setting the post in concrete—is the preferred one if you're after the best results and if time and the added cost of the concrete will permit. The hole in which the concrete is to be poured should be at least four inches wider in diameter than the post.

If the soil in which you have dug the hole is fairly firm, you can use the sides of the hole as the "form." However, if the soil is sandy, or otherwise unstable, make a form for the concrete; it's merely a four-sided open box.

The concrete mix. Use a 3:2:1 mix for the concrete (three parts of gravel or small rocks, two parts of sand, and one part of portland cement). Use a wheelbarrow, a tub, or even a large piece of plywood as a mixing "bowl."

Mix the gravel, sand, and cement thoroughly with a hoe or shovel. Make a depression in the middle of the pile and add clean water. Use the hoe to bring up the mix from the outside of the pile into the water.

Add water a little at a time, *only if necessary.* More concrete is spoiled by too much water than by too little water. The completely mixed mass should have a "heavy" consistency. Any visible water means that you have added too much. If so, add more sand and cement and *keep mixing thoroughly.*

When setting the posts, make sure that you don't force the bottoms beyond the concrete and into the earth. The concrete should be four inches above grade and sloped to drain off rain and snow.

Aligning the posts. Having set the posts in one of the four methods described, the next (and most important) step is to make sure they are in line and absolutely vertical. The first post, or corner post, is the "keystone" with which the next post should be in line. Use the string stretched between the two outside posts as a guide, and a level or a plumb bob to check the "plumb" of the post. Make this check at two adjacent sides of the post and *not at opposite sides.*

After setting each of the posts to the desired height and checking for perpendicularity and alignment, nail outrigger stakes to them to keep them in place while continuing with the rest of the job. It's best to leave the outrigger stakes in place until you have installed the horizontal parts of the fence. Leave posts set in concrete or with a concrete collar undisturbed for a week to allow the concrete to cure. Use this time to decide what style of fence you want, to order the wood, and cut it to size, if necessary.

Fence Designs

The picket fence, by far the most popular and the most traditional, is the simplest fence of all to erect. All it requires are two horizontal rails nailed to the posts, one twelve inches from the ground and the other flush with the post tops so that the tips of the pickets extend six inches above the posts.

Have you ever wondered why picket fences have pointed ends? Good looks, yes. But pointed ends shed water, preventing rot. And it's for this same reason that you should slope tops of your fence posts (see sketch below).

To ensure accurate, uniform spacing of a picket fence, use one of the pickets as a spacer. If you decide you want wider spac-

ing, simply cut a piece of scrap wood to the desired width and use it as a spacer.

There are literally dozens of other types of fences you can install, too. The drawing here de-

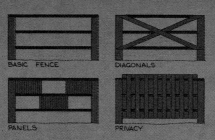

picts just a few of the designs you can select for your yard.

And there is no reason why you cannot design a fence to suit your own individual taste. Use one of the basic constructions as a springboard.

Attaching the Rails

Rail installation is just as important as post installation. Before installing the rails, paint all areas of the posts that will be in contact with them. If the fence is to be left unpainted, use a wood preservative. The paint, or preservative, will seal the crevices between the posts and rails, preventing water from seeping in and causing rot.

You can connect the rails to the posts by any of these methods:

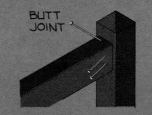

The butt joint. This is the simplest joint of all. The rails are merely toenailed to the sides of the posts as shown. Or, the rails can meet at the top of the post. It's best if you use annular or ring type nails here, as the end grain of a post has woefully little gripping power.

The lap joint. Here, the rails are nailed to the sides of the posts. A butted lap joint will be required in those situations when two rails meet. Rails should always meet at a post, not at some point between posts.

Neither the butt joint nor the lap joint requires any preparation of the posts. However, when making any of the following types of joints, prepare the posts before setting them, as it is easier to cut some of the openings beforehand rather than "in the field."

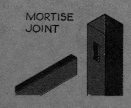

The dado joint. Cut away part of the post so that the rail will be flush (or nearly flush) with the post (as shown).

The mortise joint. This is a more elegant joint and requires cutting a hole in the post (the mortise) to accept the rail. The rails will meet at every other post to make a butt connection *inside* the mortise (assuming the posts are six feet apart and the rails are 12 feet long).

Slotted posts. This is a variation of the mortise joint (see sketch on previous page). In this case, cut the mortise high enough to accept two rails at their junction. This type of joint gives more support to the rails than the mortise joint, as part of each rail projects beyond the opening. Use this joint only at every other post.

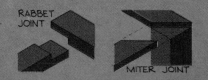

Corner joints. When the fence turns a corner, you can use any one of the above joints as well as a miter joint or a rabbet joint as indicated above.

Gates

Gates, like front doors, indicate the character of the owner and add to—or subtract from—the decor of the house. Because a gate takes a beating, pay special attention to the posts on either side. Make sure they are solidly set into the ground. As a decorative touch, they can be higher than the posts used for the rest of the fence. And the gate, incidentally, can be higher, or even lower than the fence—it's all a matter of taste.

Typical easy-to-build gates are shown in the sketch below. Note the use of cross framing to add rigidity to the gates.

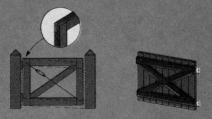

Building the gate. First of all, a gate should be a minimum of three feet wide. Construct the framework, using rabbeted lap joints at all corners (see detail in sketch above). Assemble the frame with galvanized nails, screws, or bolts. An application of waterproof glue will add to the rigidity of the gate.

Install a diagonal for bracing, or a cross brace for extra strength.

Attaching the gate. If you can attach the hinged side of the gate to a side of the house, you're halfway home because the side of

a house is excellent support for a gate. If that's not possible, you'll have to attach it to a separate post.

Hinges for brick. If you can attach your gate to the house, use the hinge shown below. This hinge is installed in the mortar between the bricks. Use a cold chisel and a hammer to make a

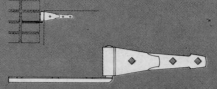

recess for the inside part of the hinge, then force a light concrete or mortar mix into the recess and around the hinge support. Let the concrete dry for a few days before installing the gate.

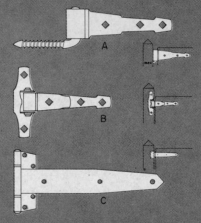

Hinges for wood. You can use any of the hinges shown above to attach hinges to a post. Hinge A has an oversize screw that is threaded into a previously drilled hole in the post. Hinge B is a decorative hinge that is secured to the fence post with two lag bolts. Hinge C is the familiar T-hinge, used for garden gates, garage and barn doors, and any other application requiring a sturdy, functional hinge.

A T-hinge actually reinforces the gate, as the long part of the T covers the gate's corner joint—always a weak area in any gate.

Installing the gate. Having decided where you want the gate and the type of hinges you're going to use, the next step is to hang the gate. First, install the hinges on the gate post (or the side of the house). Make certain that the placement of the hinges will line up with the cross rails of the gate and not at points some-

where in between.

Support the gate on some 2x4s, bricks, or anything else on hand that will raise it to the desired height. Then place the hinge leaves over the gate and mark the holes with a pencil. Drill pilot holes if you're going to use screws, and clearance holes if the job calls for bolts. Use washers under the nuts.

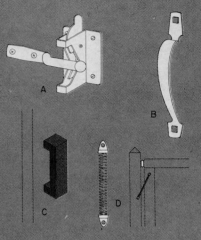

Latches, handles, and springs. In addition to hinges, a gate will require a latch and some sort of handle. Latch A (above) is self-closing. As the gate swings shut, the latch on the post engages the hardware on the gate, effectively keeping the gate closed and preventing it from rattling during a windstorm. Handle B is a store-bought variation of handle A. However, you also can make your own out of some pieces of scrap wood (handle C).

Regardless of whether or not the gate has a latch, a spring to keep it closed is always a good investment. Simply mount it as shown in D, and adjust it for fast or slow closure.

Gate stop. A simple, yet effective door stop will help prevent the hinges from loosening. You can make it from a strip of wood.

Then, simply screw it to the latch side of the gate. To silence the "bump", you can either line the inside of the strip with some rubber padding or attach a couple of rubber bumpers.